Clara's Country Year

Clara's Country Year

by Ralph Whitlock

illustrated by Shirley McLaughlin

FREDERICK WARNE

First published 1981 by Frederick Warne (Publishers) Ltd, London

ISBN 0 7232 2766 7

Filmset and printed by BAS Printers
Limited, Over Wallop, Hampshire
1508 . 1180

Contents

Introduction

In this book Clara is ten years old. She is living in the first half of the nineteenth century, about 140 years ago. Like many people in those days she is living on a farm in a village.

She shares the big farmhouse with her father and mother, her grandfather and grandmother, her brother Giles (who is twelve), her young Uncle George (who is about eighteen and her father's youngest brother) and her Aunt Martha; together with Toby the dog, and a dozen or so cats. Nearby live her Uncle Bart and Aunt Miriam, her Uncle Jonah and Aunt Tillie, and her Uncle Luther, who is a bachelor. All of them work on the same farm; Uncle Jonah looks after the sheep and Uncle Bart is the chief ploughman. In addition, the farm employs Eli, James, Little Tom and old Peter.

The farm is just outside the village of Cowbourne St George, which is situated about four miles from the market town of Norchester. Clara knows everyone in the village, where she and Giles attend the church school. Her best friends are Sarah, whose father lives at Lodge Farm, and Emmie, whose father is the blacksmith. Giles' friends are Stephen Harrasmith, Jim Mettish and

Dickie Vell. Mr Purdle, the sexton, is Giles' special enemy.

There are, of course, no motor cars. All the work on the farms is done by horses, and the vehicles on the muddy roads are all drawn by horses. Very few people except those who live there ever visit the village. Even railway trains have not yet come to this part of England. When old Peter goes to his daughter's house, forty miles away, he has to go by carriers' carts. No postman calls at the houses and there are no telephones, no radio or television, no electricity and no water taps. The houses are lit by oil lamps and candles, and old Peter spends much of his time drawing buckets of water from the well.

The people who live in the village know little about what goes on in the world outside, but they do not mind. They have plenty to keep them busy in the daily and seasonal routine of farm life. Each day all the farm animals have to be fed and kept clean and comfortable. In

February lambs are born and in March and April corn is sown. Summer sees the making of hay, followed by the corn harvest and the fruit harvest, then the fields are ploughed and the cycle begins again.

No-one goes away on holiday. Holidays take the form of festivals linked with events on the farm. In January the apple trees are wassailed, to encourage them to bear a good crop of fruit. In February, when hen's eggs are plentiful, pancakes are made and a pancake race is run. May Day and Midsummer are joyous festivals when everyone goes to the green woods to gather greenery and flowers. The coming of harvest is celebrated by Lammas-tide, a festival of first-fruits. The end of the corn harvest, which is the climax of the year, is celebrated by a Harvest Home Supper in the great barn.

Michaelmas is the season of autumn fairs, when livestock is sold or when people change jobs. By Hallowe'en the days have grown short and the nights long, so it is fun to be outdoors on a dark evening, dancing around bonfires and carrying grotesque lanterns. Christmas is a time for indoor parties, when it is pleasant to sit by a log fire while frost or snow prevails outside. The New Year sees the triumph of light over darkness; from this point the days will steadily increase in length and the sun will return.

Clara was fortunate. She lived at a time when all these things were remembered. Now many of them are forgotten or recorded only in books, and few farms like her father's survive. It must have been fun when parents, grandparents, children, aunts, uncles and neighbours were all working together on the farm. Certainly Clara enjoyed it.

Although farming is now very different, some of the features of the countryside are the same as those that Clara knew. Lambs are born in February. In March seed corn is sown in the fields. Cuckoos and swallows arrive in April, and primroses, violets and anemones open their petals in the woods. Oak-apples are to be found on oak leaves on May Day; the golden St John's wort is still in bloom on the Feast Day of St John the Baptist, which is midsummer.

So, throughout the year, if you are lucky enough to live in the country or to be able to visit it regularly, you may see many of the things that Clara saw. For the rest, you must close your eyes and use your imagination. It will be easier for you to do so than it would have been for Clara to imagine herself in your world. She could never have imagined radio or television or telephones or electricity or cars or aeroplanes or men visiting the moon. Was she the lucky one or are you?

1 *January*

Wassailing the Apple Trees

When her grandmother said, 'The wind is blowing the rain away. It will be fine for the wassailing tonight,' Clara was delighted. Wassailing the apple trees was fun on a cold, sparkling night, when the stars glittered as though Aunt Martha had spent hours polishing them, but rain, like last year's, spoiled it all. Clara stared out of the window at the low, grey clouds still racing across the sky like the dust billowing out of the barn door when old Peter was sweeping the barn floor, knowing that her father was not far away, but she could see no sign of the fine weather that her granny promised. But Granny knew best. She was always right.

'Up to your room, Clara, and bring down a bucket of apples—the eating ones on the ledge by the window,' ordered her grandmother.

Clara went willingly. She and her grandmother understood each other very well. All the other women, busy with preparations in the kitchen, had no time for small girls at present, but Granny knew that she was longing to help.

Ever since she could remember Clara had had to share her bedroom—the little end room with sloping ceilings, tucked high under the roof—with apples. In October and November apples overflowed everywhere. Big heaps were piled on straw in the barn loft; more apples filled the cupboard under the stairs; and the best ones were stored in the bedrooms. Clara's father and mother had the floor of their room covered with boxes filled with apples, so did her grandfather and grandmother, and so did her Uncle George. There weren't enough boxes to use in Giles' and Clara's rooms, so the apples were just laid on the floor. Clara, carrying a candlestick in one hand, had to tread carefully along a narrow path between a carpet of apples when she went to bed every night. Apples extended in an unbroken layer under the bed, too, where they accumulated a thick layer of dust and fluff that had to be wiped off before they could be used. These were big green apples that were used whole, for apple dumplings. The eating apples, all rosy and glowing, sat in rows on the window ledge. Clara used to eat one whenever she wanted to; there were plenty, and nobody minded.

Staggering back into the kitchen with a bucketful of apples almost heavier than she could carry she bumped into fussy Aunt Martha, who was bustling about as usual without achieving much.

'Oh, get out of the way, child, do!' exclaimed Aunt Martha. '*Must* you come in here when we're so busy?'

Before Clara had thought of what to say she was gone. Granny was nowhere in sight, so Clara parked the bucket at one end of the tall, warped wooden sideboard, where no-one was likely to fall over it, and retreated to her grandfather's chair by the fire. It was the most comfortable chair in the kitchen, having an old red cushion on the hard wooden seat. Samkin, the black-and-white cat, knew that too, and was already in residence. He purred for a few moments when Clara lifted him up to sit on her lap but soon resumed his nap.

The trays of scones, pastries, pies and lardy cakes were accumulating with fascinating speed under the deft hands of Clara's mother, aided to some extent by fluttery Aunt Martha, fetching and carrying between kitchen and scullery. Clara would have liked to join in but knew better than to interrupt her preoccupied mother, who had no time for small girls when she was really busy. So she waited until her grandmother reappeared.

'Toast,' said her grandmother, who was good at finding things for Clara to do. 'Come on, Clara, you can toast some bread from where you're sitting. We shall need some for the robins tonight.'

So Clara sat with Samkin on her lap and toasted slices of home-made bread over the glowing fire. She had to extend the wire toasting-fork to its limit, and even then she had to wind her handkerchief around her hand, to protect it from the heat.

The men came in from milking at five o'clock, and it was half-past six before tea had been cleared away (not a big tea tonight, because there was a feast to follow) and everybody had changed into better clothes. Not Sunday going-to-meetings clothes, but the clothes they wore when they went to market. Good, plain, serviceable clothes, but clean.

Soon the rest of the family arrived. There were Uncle Jonah and Aunt Tillie, Uncle Bart and Aunt Miriam, and Uncle Luther. Clara liked Aunt Miriam, who was small, not much taller than Clara herself, and had brown dancing eyes. She was a little afraid of tall, stately Aunt Tillie, who held herself so erect and talked like a schoolteacher.

Grand-dad, who had put on his red waistcoat and had his huge watch-chain festooned across it, drew a mug of cider for each one, and they all stood around chatting till the last visitors had arrived. These were Eli, James, Little Tom and Peter, the men who worked on the farm. They were given mugs of cider, too, from the barrel mounted on a stool just inside the door. Clara could not make up her mind whether they continued standing near the door because they thought it was their proper place or because they wanted to be near the barrel when it was time for second helpings. They had all brought musical instruments with them. Little Tom's was particularly conspicuous because it was a drum so big that it was taller than his waist when he rested it on the floor. Old Peter had his fiddle, and Eli and James carried their cornets or trumpets.

'Well, are we ready?' enquired Grand-dad, and without waiting for an answer went across to the gun-rack and took down the muzzle-loading gun that he used for shooting rabbits. The uncles went to fetch their guns which they had left in the porch, except for Uncle Luther, who carried a strange, wiggly instrument called a 'serpent' which he had borrowed from Clara's grandfather and which he was learning to play. Clara thought that the low, moaning sound it made wasn't very musical, but perhaps that was because Uncle Luther couldn't play it very well yet.

'You'd better have your gloves on to start with,' Granny told her, helping her on with her thick, blue overcoat with the rabbit fur around the neck.

The other women were arming themselves with tin trays, pans and kettles, and with pokers and fire-irons to beat them, but Clara knew that she wouldn't need any. As the youngest member of the family she had her own important part to play.

Grandfather looked around to make sure everybody was present. It was absolutely essential that the whole family be there, or the spells would not work. Two or three years ago when Giles had measles they had got him out of bed and wrapped him up warmly in blankets, so that he should not miss the ceremony.

'Right,' said Grandfather, and out into the cold darkness they all trooped.

The yellow light of the lanterns helped them to avoid the worst patches of mud as they picked their way across the yard but formed only a small pool of light in the black world. There was no moon that night, and most of the stars were hidden by clouds. A horse whinnied as they passed the stables, and in the warm cowsheds cows clanked their chains as they fidgeted, sounds so familiar that Clara took little notice of them.

In the orchard they plodded to the biggest tree of all, the old Tom Putt tree that grew in the corner nearest the smithy, which its branches overhung.

'Come, Clara,' said her grandfather, and her mother pushed her forward. While all the others gathered in a circle around the gnarled old trunk, their faces golden in the lantern light, Grand-dad picked her up in his arms and held her close to the tree. Her father followed and gave her an earthenware jug of cider which he had been carrying, and Granny handed her a slice of toast.

Clara knew what she had to do. She dipped the toast in the cider and held it there for a moment, until it was thoroughly soaked. Then she wedged it into a fork of the tree, where one of the biggest branches curved away from the trunk.

'Wedge it in tight,' commanded her grandmother, 'so that the robins can find it in the morning.'

Her grandfather lowered her to the ground and straightened himself. Clara then poured all the cider left in the jug over the trunk of the tree.

As she stepped back she pressed her hands to her ears, for she knew what would happen next. Her grandfather, father and uncles had raised their guns and, at a signal from Grand-dad, they discharged a volley up through the branches towards the dark sky. At the same time, the women began beating their trays, pans and kettles, making as much noise as they could.

'That's to make sure the spirits of the apple trees are paying proper

attention to what we have been doing,' her grandmother had told her.

The din woke the bull in his shed by the farmyard. He bellowed once or twice, and some of the cows answered. Far away in the woods cock pheasants called in alarm.

Before they had finished, the improvised band got to work. After a few tentative chords from old Peter's fiddle they launched into the Wassailing Song, and, after the first line, everybody joined in heartily,

Old Apple Tree, Old Apple Tree,
We wassail thee, and hope that thou wilt bear;
For the Lord doth know where we shall be
Till apples come another year;
For to bear well and to bloom well,
So merry let us be,
Let every man take off his hat and shout to thee,
Old Apple Tree, Old Apple Tree,
We wassail thee and hope that thou wilt bear
Hat fulls
Cap fulls
Three bushel bag fulls,
And a little heap under the stairs.

As the last chords died away, Grand-dad raised his arm, waved his hat and shouted, 'Hip-hip-' and everyone yelled 'Hooray!' This happened three times.

'We'd best wassail another one for luck,' said Grand-dad, so they went on to another large tree and repeated the performance.

This time, though, as the song came to an end, Granny seized Clara by the hand and hurried her back towards the house. All the other women were running, too. Having only one lantern, which Aunt Tillie was carrying well ahead, those at the rear slipped on the mud and splashed through puddles. They hardly noticed it, though, as their one thought was to get home before the men. Clara and her grandmother were last, of course, because Granny couldn't run as fast as the younger ones, but eventually they were safely in the kitchen and Mother was locking and bolting the door.

'Now, what shall it be this year?' asked Clara's mother, rosy-cheeked and breathing heavily.

They had to place something, something that wouldn't normally be there, on the hearth, and the men, locked outside the door, would not be admitted till they guessed what it was.

Last year it had been Mother's hair-brush.

'Let's try Grand-dad's top-hat,' suggested Aunt Miriam, gaily.

'I don't think that Grand-dad would approve of that, somehow,' remarked Granny, doubtfully.

Aunt Martha, looking around and mentioning the first object that caught her eye, suggested moving the grandfather clock, but no-one even bothered to answer her.

'The sheep-shearing shears,' said Mother.

'My hat,' said Aunt Tillie.

'How about the cream jug?' enquired Granny.

Eventually it was decided that it would be the cream jug. It was a delicate piece of pottery, painted with pictures of milkmaids, and the men would never think of that being placed on the hearth.

They were hammering on the door now, banging with their fists and shouting loudly. One of them gave a blast on his trumpet.

'All right, all right, we can hear you,' Mother called. 'Start guessing.'

'Toast.'

'My boots.'

'The kettle.'

'Miriam's nightdress,' said her husband.

'The Bible.'

Guesses came thick and fast, often two or three being shouted at the same time.

'We give in,' yelled a voice. 'It's starting to snow.'

'Keep guessing,' the women called back. 'Keep guessing.'

'A feather duster.'

'No.'

'A powder flask.'

'No.'

'Samkin,' came Giles's voice.

'No.'

'Yes—yes!' put in Clara, suddenly. 'Look!'

They all turned to see Samkin with his head in the cream-jug, licking out the last drops.

'Oh, my goodness!' exclaimed Clara's mother, 'Samkin!'

'That dratted cat!' said her grandmother. 'I'll skin him!'

But Samkin, after a last hurried lick, had retreated under the sideboard, where he was safe for a time.

'Hey! What's happening? Let us in!' came the shouts from outside, with renewed hammering on the door.

'Let them in, before they break down the door,' commanded Granny, and Aunt Miriam slid back the bolts and turned the great key. The men trooped in, with snow flecking their coats, and demanded to know why they had been kept waiting. Explanations were made, and everyone crowded to warm up around the huge log fire burning on the hearth.

Over it simmered an enormous pot of cider—mulled cider it was called—into which Granny had stirred some brown sugar, raisins, nutmeg and spices. Everyone had a steaming mug of it, even Clara, though her mother insisted on adding some water to hers.

'Here's to the old apple tree,' called Grand-dad, raising his mug, and they all drank another toast to the apple trees. Then everyone had to eat one of those red, juicy apples that Clara had brought down from her bedroom.

'Well, that's the wassailing done for another year,' said Grand-dad, with satisfaction. 'That'll make sure the trees will bear a good crop again, eh, Peter?'

'Aye,' agreed Peter.

'Wouldn't they have any apples if they weren't wassailed?' asked Clara.

'How can we tell?' retorted her grandmother. 'We've *always* wassailed them, ever since I can remember, and ever since *my* grandmother could remember. It has to be done on the right night, too, otherwise it won't work. It must be on the Eve of Old Twelfth Night.'

'What's Old Twelfth Night, Gran?'

'It's the Twelfth Night after Christmas, according to the old reckoning, before the calendar was changed, and that happened nearly a hundred years ago. Anyway, it's 16 January, that's all you need to remember. And mind you *do* remember it.'

'Oh, I will,' Clara assured her. 'I wouldn't want to forget about wassailing, it's fun.'

2 *February*

Lambs and Pancakes

'Today is Candlemas Day,' Clara's granny told her. 'Today we have tea before we light the lamps.'

It was tea-time on 2 February, and the days were growing longer. On the shortest day (21 December) the sun had sunk below the horizon behind the big beech tree on the hill, but now it was setting by the old cattle shed, one field farther north. What interested Clara more was that at sunset its rays were now reflected in the mirror on the sideboard opposite her place at the table. The mirror had cut-glass edges, one of which reflected a rainbow of light across the table to Clara's plate. By moving her hand Clara could make it green, blue, red, yellow—in fact, all the colours of the rainbow.

'When I was a boy I used to sit in that place,' her father told her, 'and I knew that when I could make rainbows on my hand spring was on the way.'

'I heard a blackbird singing this morning,' he added.

'That's early,' said Clara's mother.

'Too early,' said her grandfather, shaking his head with foreboding. 'It isn't spring yet, not by many a long week. We used to say, "On the farm on Candlemas Day there should be half the straw and half the hay".'

'Well, we're all right,' said her father cheerfully. 'We've got plenty in the barn.'

'That proverb means that we should have half the winter food for the cattle and sheep still uneaten,' he explained to Clara and Giles. 'It means that the winter is no more than half over.'

'There's another saying—"As the day lengthens, so the cold strengthens",' said Grand-dad gloomily. 'You mark my words, we've got some hard weather to come.'

'Good!' exclaimed Giles. 'Will it be hard enough for us to go skating?'

But no-one answered him.

So far most of the winter had been mild. There had been frosts in early December and a snowstorm on 16 January, but after a few days rain had washed the snow away and it seemed to have been raining ever since.

'I wish to goodness we could have a few weeks of fine weather. I'd rather have frost than this,' grumbled Uncle Jonah, whose special job was to look after the sheep. He had two hundred ewes (female sheep) due to produce their lambs in February and he was growing anxious about them. The thick woolly coats that protect sheep against frost and cold winds become very heavy and uncomfortable when they get wet. When they are continually wet the sheep sometimes catch chills; or when they roll over on their backs they are unable to get up again if their fleeces are too heavy. Uncle Jonah and Uncle Luther, who was helping him at this important season, walked around the flock, inspecting every sheep, several times a day.

They and several of the other men were also busy building a lambing pen. They chose a site in the corner of a field, with high hedges on the north and east sides, as a shelter from cold winds. On the west side a rick of straw had been made, so that the pen was open only to the south.

'If there *is* any sunshine, we shall trap it,' said Uncle Jonah.

With wattle hurdles they made a big square pen. When it was finished they divided it into four quarters with more hurdles. The two outer compartments were for the sheep and lambs after the lambing was safely over. One of the others was for the sheep before they had their lambs. The final one, tucked comfortably against the straw rick, had a row of tiny pens around every side. Each was just large enough for one sheep and her lamb. Its sides were built of two hurdles, about two feet apart with straw stuffed between the two, to keep out draughts. Other hurdles were placed on the top and thatched with straw. The result was a delightfully snug little den.

'As each lamb is born we put it, with its mother, into one of these little pens,' Uncle Jonah explained to Clara. 'It stays there for about two days, after which it should be strong enough to go out and join the flock.'

Near the pens, but not too near the straw rick, Uncle Jonah had a shepherd's hut. This was a kind of wooden house on wheels, where Uncle Jonah would live for four or five weeks while the sheep were having their lambs. Along one side was a bed with plenty of blankets but no sheets.

'I'll lie there and have naps for a few hours at a time,' Uncle Jonah grinned, 'but I shan't take my clothes off, as I'll have to get up at intervals all through the night to attend to any lambs that have been born. Most of them seem to be born at night, worse luck!'

He also had a stove with an oven, so that he could warm up the food which Aunt Tillie sent for him. On a shelf were cans and bottles of sheep medicines, and on another were mugs, plates and cutlery. An oil lamp and lantern hung from nails. There were a table, a rocking chair and some pegs for Uncle Jonah to hang his smock, his coat and his hat on. In one corner was a heap of split logs, which was replenished from a much larger one outside.

'I keep a fire going in the stove day and night,' Uncle Jonah told Clara. 'It gets as hot as an oven in here, but that's nice when it's frosty outside.'

Clara rather envied Uncle Jonah. She thought she would like to camp out in a little hut like that, though she would want to make it tidier and more comfortable. Her granny laughed when she confided in her.

'Men are seldom tidy, and they don't know how to make

themselves comfortable,' she said. 'That's what we women are for!'

From observation Clara had already realized that that was so, in her family.

Uncle Jonah went up to the lambing-pen to live in his hut on 12 February and three days later the first lambs were born. On the Saturday, when she did not have to go to school, Clara went up to see them. Each lamb was warm and snug with its mother in one of the little thatched pens, and Uncle Jonah was feeling cheerful.

'We hardly need to tuck them in like this, as long as this weather lasts,' he observed.

The sun was shining, the wind was in the south, and the hazel bushes in the hedges were hung with myriads of catkins—'lamb's-tails' Clara called them, because they were so much like the dangling woolly tails of the lambs.

Now that he was living in his hut Uncle Jonah had another little shed nearby. It was fitted into a corner and had an open courtyard of hurdles in front of it, with wire-netting laid over the top. Peeping in to see what lived there, Clara found herself looking at five or six brown hens, all with the bright eyes and red combs which indicated they were ready to lay.

'They provide my breakfast,' Uncle Jonah twinkled. 'And on Tuesday I'm going to make myself some pancakes!'

'Is it Pancake Day on Tuesday?' Clara asked her granny when she arrived home.

'Bless me, so it is!' Granny exclaimed, 'and I'd forgotten. Still, I expect someone else would have remembered.'

'Is it the same day every year?' Clara enquired.

'No, it depends on Easter. The forty days before Easter is the season of Lent, when, a long time ago, people used to fast. That begins on Ash Wednesday, which is next Wednesday. The day before that is Shrove Tuesday, or Pancake Day.'

'Why?'

'Well, I expect that when people were about to spend forty days fasting they liked to have a good feast before they started. And there would be plenty of eggs about at this time of the year to make pancakes with, even if there wasn't much meat.'

'Did people really fast for forty days, Granny?'

'No, it wasn't a complete fast, but they went without meat and all sorts of luxuries, such as pancakes.'

On Tuesday morning Clara's mother and her aunts joined with other women of the village in the annual village pancake race. They lined up with their frying pans and pancakes outside the Bull and Billet and raced along the street to the church. Each competitor had to toss the pancake and catch it in the pan three times as she ran. Many of them were not quick enough and dropped their pancakes in the mud.

Mrs Harrasmith, Stephen's mother, won the race and Clara's Aunt Miriam came second.

'I'm glad Mrs Harrasmith came in first,' said Aunt Miriam. 'With seven children to feed she can do with the prize.'

The prize was a sack of flour and a dozen eggs. It was presented to

Mrs Harrasmith by the vicar in the church porch, where immediately afterwards the children had their egg-shackling contest. Clara, like all the other children, had brought an egg, on which she had written her name. She placed it with the others in a big sieve on the porch floor. Then the vicar picked up the sieve and began to shake it gently. One after another the eggs cracked, until there were only three left. Clara's was one.

The vicar vibrated the sieve again. The eggs rolled about and cannoned into each other. One cracked completely in half, the contents running out through the mesh of the sieve. It bore the name of Clara's friend, Emmie. The vicar inspected the other two closely.

'This one's cracked,' he announced, holding it up to the light.

The one that was left was Clara's. Everyone clapped when the vicar declared Clara the winner of the egg-shackling contest. She had to walk up and receive a sheet of stiff paper which was called a certificate. It said that she was entitled to first prize.

'But what *is* first prize?' she asked her granny when she returned to the crowd, clutching the paper.

Granny laughed, 'You'd never guess.'

'Why?'

'It's one of your Uncle Jonah's lambs! We've given an orphan lamb for a prize, and whoever wins it will bring it up on a bottle. But you'll have to wait till we get an orphan lamb. There isn't one yet.'

Clara was delighted at first, but after she had thought about it she was not so sure.

'I would love to have a lamb,' she told her granny, 'but I don't think I want it to be an orphan. That would mean its mother had died.'

'These things happen every year,' said Granny. 'But often a ewe has two lambs or even three and can't feed them all. Then one has to be taken away and reared on the bottle. Maybe you can have one of those.'

Two nights later the mild south-westerly breeze faded away, and in the morning a bitterly cold wind was blowing from the east.

'We shall have snow,' Clara's father predicted.

Sure enough, as the short day faded into twilight, light snowflakes began to fall. At first there were only a few, but when Clara looked out of the back door just before she went to bed a curtain of snow was swirling past.

'It's the sort of snow that keeps on and on,' said her father gloomily.

Clara thought of Uncle Jonah in his little hut in the lambing pen and hoped he was keeping warm.

Next day the snow stopped for a few hours and the men were able to attend to the needs of all the farm animals, but in the evening it started again, worse than before. As they sat by the fire in the evening Clara's family could hear the wind howling and shrieking outside, rattling the windows and occasionally dropping a flurry of snowflakes down the chimney, to sizzle on the burning logs.

'It's a real blizzard,' said her father. 'We shall have trouble tomorrow.'

When Clara looked out of her bedroom window the next morning the world was dazzling white. The storm had passed and the sun shone weakly from a pale blue sky. She could hear sounds of a shovel scraping on stones not far away, and, looking down, she saw old Peter shovelling snow from the courtyard. A space had already been cleared around the back door, but a snowdrift was piled against the woodshed door higher than the latch. A bright-eyed robin was perched on a broom-handle and eyeing old Peter with interest, hoping for a breakfast.

'I must go down and feed him,' thought Clara, scrambling into her clothes.

But when she threw out some scraps for the robin, hosts of other hungry birds, especially a mob of noisy starlings, descended on the meal, so Clara had to give them a second helping, to make sure that the robin got enough. She kept a watchful eye on the door to see that no cats came leaping out, but the cats, having had their breakfast, were curled up by the fire.

Clara was lucky. There was no school for her on Saturdays.

About mid-morning, after she had helped with the washing-up and the other Saturday morning chores, Clara was just wondering what would be the best excuse to get outdoors in the snow when

Giles, her brother, came in. He had been cleaning out the calf pens and putting fresh straw into the poultry barn, and now he announced, 'I'm going up to the sheep-fold. Are you coming, Clara?'

Clara's mother raised no objection, so, putting on their warmest clothes, they set off.

It was hard going. All the roads and lanes were filled with snow to the very tops of the hedges. It was impossible to walk in them. Where the wind had swept the snow through gaps in the hedges or around the corners of buildings there were drifts of fantastic shapes. Some of the drifts were like enormous curling waves, like the waves at the seaside just as they are about to break.

'The only way to get through them would be to tunnel,' said Giles.

However, the wind during the night had been so strong that it had swept some of the exposed fields almost bare. So Clara and Giles walked across the fields, keeping well away from the hedges.

At the sheepfold they found their father, Uncle Bart and Uncle Luther as well as Uncle Jonah. They too had been busy with shovels and had cleared away snow from around the shepherd's hut and some of the pens.

'Are all the lambs all right?' asked Giles.

'I shouldn't worry your Uncle Jonah,' Uncle Luther advised them. 'He's grumpy. He's been up all night.'

'Did he lose any lambs?'

'No, he doesn't think so. There were eight of them born in the blizzard, though. It's a wonder some didn't die.'

Clara peeped into some of the little straw huts and saw that they had been cleared of snow and littered with fresh straw. The mother and lamb inside each seemed cosy and warm.

'Yes, they're all right,' Uncle Luther agreed. 'But we think some more may be buried under the deep snow by the hurdles. We're going to start digging there in a minute or two.'

As there were no spades or shovels for them to use, Giles and Clara thought they would do better to keep out of the way. They peeped inside the hut, where Uncle Jonah's breakfast plate and cup were still on the table. On the stove stood a big box of hay.

'I wonder what that's for?' said Clara.

As she spoke Uncle Jonah came in. Reaching under his smock he pulled out a limp lamb which appeared to be dead.

'Here's another one to join the crowd,' he grunted. Taking down the box he dug deep into the hay, hollowed a kind of nest in it and dropped the lamb in.

'There's two in there already,' he observed. 'That makes three.'

He covered the lamb with hay, pressed it down tightly and replaced the box on the hot stove. Clara was alarmed.

'But won't it suffocate? Won't it roast?' she cried.

'All three of those lambs will be jumping about this hut like lively fleas before dark tonight,' he assured her. 'Now go and see if you can be of help somewhere. This hut is getting too crowded.'

The other men were still digging in the snow, aided by two dogs, neither of which was Toby.

'I wonder where *he* is?' said Giles and then almost immediately saw him running backwards and forwards at the far side of one of the pens. At least, he was trying to run but as he came near the hurdles the snow was so deep that he floundered in it up to his stomach. He was barking with frustration.

'Let's go and help him,' suggested Giles. 'He looks as though he's found the scent of something. A rabbit, I expect.'

When they reached him, though, they found the weight of the snow had pushed over one of the hurdles which formed the wall of the pen. Clara and Giles helped him over the deepest snow, and immediately he started following a scent track across the field. The snow had covered any footprints, but Toby had a keen nose and went racing towards the next hedge, a long way ahead. Clara and Giles followed as fast as they could.

Just before they reached the hedge they came to an old chalk-pit—a depression from which chalk had once been dug. Bushes and trees were now growing in it, and everything was deep in snow. Toby plunged in and, after sniffing around for a minute or two, selected a giant snow-drift and started to dig.

'I supposed we'd better go and help the silly old dog,' Giles said, 'though he'll never get a rabbit out from under all that snow.'

Toby kept barking and digging frantically, so they helped him as best they could by shovelling with their gloved hands and trampling with their feet.

Suddenly Clara saw a tuft of wool, dirty yellowish against the pure white snow. She stooped to pick it up and found it was attached to something—a sheep!

Now Toby and the children dug faster than ever.

'It doesn't move,' said Clara. 'I think it's dead.'

And so it was. But under the ewe, still alive though cold and limp, was a newly-born lamb, with black face and ears and black feet.

Clara tucked it inside her coat, which she buttoned up again.

'Back to the hut. Quick!' shouted Giles.

They ran as fast as the snow would let them, with Toby prancing beside them, barking and jumping up to assure himself that the lamb was still there.

At the hut Uncle Jonah quickly took charge of the half-alive lamb. He rubbed it vigorously with a warm sack, massaged it with his big, horny hands and then stuffed it into the hay box.

Giles explained to him how Toby had found the sheep and lamb, and Uncle Jonah rewarded the dog with a pat.

'You *are* a good dog, Toby,' Clara told him.

Toby sat on the floor, watching the hay-box alertly. He knew what was inside.

'I'd better go and see this dead ewe,' said Uncle Jonah. 'I suppose she is dead?'

'I'm afraid so,' said Giles.

'Well, I'll go and bring her in, before the foxes get at her. We don't want them to get a taste for mutton.'

'That's the first ewe I've lost this year,' he remarked as he paused at the door. 'Can never seem to get through lambing without losing one or two. Ah well, there's one lamb will have to be reared on the bottle. Let's see, didn't somebody win one as a prize at the egg-shackling last Tuesday?'

He plodded down the steps, not looking back to see Clara's eyes shining with happiness.

3 *May*

May Day

Clara lay, half-asleep, in her bed, listening to the sounds of the countryside that came floating through the open window. Sparrows were chattering under the eaves, a starling perched on the roof of the woodshed was trying to mimic the blackbird singing from the big apple tree, and a cuckoo was calling in the distant meadows. Someone across the yard was rattling a milk bucket. A calf blared, and its mother answered. A hen cackled triumphantly as she emerged from the hen-house, after having laid an egg.

Clara's granny came out from the kitchen and started sweeping the paving-stones outside the back door, singing as she wielded the broom. This is the song she was singing:

May Day's breaking,
All the world's awaking,
Let me see the sun rise over the plain.
Why have you awoke me?
How you do provoke me!
Let me have a little time to doze off again.

Sleeping in the daytime
Wastes the happy Maytime,
Makes an empty pocket and a cloudy brain.

Clara smiled, she thought the song was intended for her because Granny was singing quite loudly and was also banging the broom against doors and buckets and making as much noise as possible.

Clara rolled out of bed, sat still for a moment and then ran across to the window.

'All right, I'm awake,' she called to her granny.

'And about time,' retorted Granny. 'Don't you know it's May Day? Everyone else has been up for hours.'

Clara thought that must be an exaggeration, for the clock on the chest of drawers said only half-past five. But then she remembered that everyone got up very early on May Day morning.

'Oh dear!' she exclaimed, hurrying to dress. 'I do hope they haven't gone without me.'

Downstairs everyone was putting on greatcoats and topboots, for even on May Day it is still cold in the early morning. Her mother poured out a cup of hot tea for Clara, who also helped herself to a bun from the cake-bin, for she knew there would be no breakfast till they returned. The May Day custom had to be observed before they sat down to a meal.

When all were ready they set off for the woods, taking the footpath which is a short cut to Druid's Lane. Clara's father, grandfather and Uncle George took the lead, each carrying a bill-hook and a rope. Her mother, grandmother and Aunt Martha were armed with pruning-shears, Giles had a pocket-knife which he kept opening and shutting, except when he was playing with Toby, who had insisted on coming. Clara had nothing to carry.

The journey along footpaths and lanes to the great woods was at least a mile. When they arrived they found many people there already, all chopping down young hazel and ash trees or cutting off branches of oaks, beeches and sycamores. The men got busy at once, collecting green boughs and saplings, while the women snipped off twigs with their shears.

'I remember coming up here with *my* grandmother when I was a little girl,' Clara's granny told her, 'and she said she used to do the same when she was small. It's a very old custom.'

Clara's task was to look for oak-apples, those round galls, like marbles, which grow on the leaves and twigs of oak-trees at this season. The person who found the branch with the largest number of oak-apples on it received a prize. Clara looked for a long time without finding one and then she came upon a tree heavily infested with the galls and she broke off a small branch with fourteen of them on it.

'That could be a prizewinner,' said her mother.

Giles was supposed to be searching for oak-apples, too, but he had wandered far into the woods, looking for birds' nests. His father had to call him back when they were ready to go home.

'Come on, my lad. You can take some of these branches if you've nothing else to carry,' said Grand-dad.

'Serve you right for birds'-nesting,' Clara taunted him. 'See what I've got,' and she showed him her oak-apples.

'Phoo, that's nothing,' Giles replied. 'I could find more than that without even looking.'

He jumped to grab the nearest oak-branch, broke off the end of it, and passed it to Clara to inspect. The leaves were covered with oak-apples. Together they counted them—fifteen! Clara was so vexed she could have hit him.

Some of the branches the men had cut were too heavy to carry and had to be dragged along by ropes. The men had to do it themselves; they weren't allowed to use horses. That was one of the old May Day rules. They could go to the woods before breakfast on May Day morning and cut whatever green branches they could carry or drag along, but even hand-carts were forbidden.

Skylarks were unwinding their silvery chain of song overhead as they trudged back towards the village. Peewits wheeled and shouted with alarm when they thought anyone was approaching too near to their nests in the open fields. The lambs, still with their mothers, were now growing fast and prancing about in the green meadows. Every field, every hedgerow, every tree was now a vivid emerald green.

The lace-like cow parsley on the hedge banks seemed to reflect the little puffy white clouds sailing overhead.

'The grass is growing well this spring,' remarked Grand-dad.

'Yes, it's time we put the heifers out to graze. We'll do it presently,' agreed Clara's father.

The heifers were young cattle, born in the previous year, which had been spending the winter in covered yards. May Day was considered the proper day for turning them loose in the pastures, where they would live on grass all the summer.

'We can move them between events this afternoon,' said Grand-dad.

Hauling the bigger branches along the paths and narrow lanes to the village was a back-breaking task, but big ones were needed to decorate the houses. When the decorations were finished some of the cottages were so hidden by greenery that they looked more like a forest than houses. A specially large branch was hauled, by means of a pulley, to the pinnacle of the church tower, where it hung beneath the red cross flag of St George. Some householders tied bouquets or fixed vases of flowers to the branches they had collected, and fixed garlands to the doors, for prizes were awarded for the best decorated houses.

Before the task was completed Clara and Giles felt that it was long past breakfast-time. At last they were called in and each given a plate of rashers, two fried eggs and fried bread.

'Nothing like a two-mile walk before breakfast to give you an appetite,' grinned their father, as they wolfed it down, following the first course with bread and honey.

'Don't be too long,' Granny said to Clara. 'It'll soon be time for the procession.'

Clara didn't need reminding, for this year she was to be one of the May Queen's attendants. The May Queen was usually a thirteen-year-old girl (this year it was Gwen Pothecary), so it might be Clara's turn in a few years' time. It would be nice to sit at the side of the May Queen on the waggon and hear all the people cheering, Clara thought. Aunt Miriam had made, for her and the other two attendants, pretty dresses of white and gold, with garlands for head-dresses, and they had posies and green parasols, trimmed with lace, to carry.

Grand-dad took Clara down to the village green in the pony-trap, so that she wouldn't get her dress dirty. Even the pony and trap were decorated with greenery, and Gipsy, the pony, wore her best polished harness and had a bunch of cowslips fixed in the centre of her bridle.

A crowd of people had already gathered on the green outside the churchyard wall when they arrived. The May Queen's waggon was so completely covered by a green rick-cloth that even the wheels were hidden. The throne was an upright armchair, buried in green branches. Two smaller chairs, one on either side, were for two of the attendants, Mary Grey and Janet Mettish, while Clara, the smallest attendant, had to curl up on a cushion at the queen's feet. Someone had thoughtfully brought some steps, so that the girls could climb easily onto the platform. The waggon was to be drawn by two giant Shire horses, named Major and Colonel, lent by Mr Garrett of Manor Farm. They too were arrayed in glittering harness, complete with highly polished horse-brasses and sets of brass bells which chimed and tinkled whenever the horses moved. They were magnificent.

As Clara climbed on the waggon and settled down on her cushion, the band arrived. Most of them were dressed in red and blue uniforms, though some of the new recruits wore their Sunday-best clothes. They carried cornets, trumpets, trombones and other brass instruments, with the big drum, beaten by Little Tom, to keep them in time. While they were getting into line and testing their instruments, other villagers in fancy dress took up their positions behind the May Queen's chariot. The children came first, many of them dressed as fairy-story characters, and then the young men and girls. Some wore their Sunday clothes, but many of the young men had green knee-breeches, white shirts, cross-gartered stockings and straw hats, while the girls were dressed in green skirts and bodices with white blouses. It was a symphony of green and white, matching the green and white of the countryside. Billy Shammick was disguised as a sweep, his face and hands covered with soot. ('A sweep is supposed to bring good luck,' said Clara's granny.) Clara's Uncle George had squeezed inside a Hobby Horse, which was an ugly image in the shape of a horse. It had a movable neck, great glaring eyes, and jaws which worked up and down by pulling a string. Uncle George intended to have fun, prancing about in the procession and trying to bite the girls who were watching.

When all were ready the band started a lively tune and the procession moved off. It marched along the High Street, turned right by the pond, and circled the village by way of the back road, arriving back at the churchyard gate half-an-hour later. There the fancy dresses were judged, the May Queen was crowned by Lady FitzAppleton who lived at The Hall, and the prizes presented. Clara couldn't help smiling when Giles didn't get a prize for his oak-apples after all. Stephen Harrasmith's little sister, Margaret, had a branch with eighteen on it.

Passing through the village, on their way home for their midday meal, Clara's family was accosted by Mr Purdle, the sexton. Mr Purdle lived in a tumbledown cottage with a large, weedy garden and an old orchard attached to it. The far side of the orchard adjoined Clara's father's land.

Mr Purdle sidled out from the garden gate and stood in the road, so that Clara's father had to stop to speak to him.

'You'll be moving the heifers out to grass presently, I expect,' said Mr Purdle. 'It'll be all right for me to put mine with them as usual, I dare say?'

'I suppose so,' Clara's father replied, looking none too pleased.

'He does that every year,' he commented, as they walked on, 'and he always forgets to pay.'

'And he'll always do it until one year you say "no",' said Clara's mother.

'I haven't the heart to. He hasn't any meadows of his own . . . only that little orchard. And after all, it's only one heifer.'

'Which he's been keeping at your expense all the winter, I dare say,' retorted Clara's mother. 'How many trusses of hay has he "borrowed" this winter?'

'Well, I suppose he has had a few,' Clara's father admitted.

'And forgotten to pay for them, I'll be bound. Joshua Purdle has a wonderful memory for "forgetting".'

The May Day festivities were resumed at about three o'clock in the afternoon. By that time everybody on the farms, except for those who had cows to milk, had finished the necessary work for the day. Most of the women were busy in the church hall, preparing the May Day feast, which would be ready at about six o'clock. The carcasses of three sheep were being roasted on spits over outdoor fires.

'These feasts used to be called "Church Ales",' Clara's granny told her. 'I suppose it was because they used to drink ale instead of tea in those days.'

Clara noticed, though, that there were still a dozen or so casks of ale or cider piled against a wall at the back of the hall.

'In the old days,' her granny continued, 'the vicar was supposed to provide all the food and drink. But that would have been so expensive for the poor man that people used to give him money and things to help out. Now we have a fund to which everyone contributes.'

The younger men and girls were dancing on the village green. Some of the dances, which everyone joined in, were just jigs, but the village had some expert dancers who knew the steps of the old Morris dances. These were performed to the music of an accordion and two fiddles and were very lively. At times the dancers leapt high into the air, shouting loudly and banging their cudgels together. One very complicated dance was performed with wooden swords. It finished with the leader kneeling in the middle of a ring of dancers who had deftly arranged their swords in a star-shaped pattern around his neck so that he couldn't move.

That was a very energetic dance, so when it was finished the dancers had a rest while the children danced around the maypole. In the middle of the village green lay a large stone, the centre of which had been carved out to take the base of a tall pole. This maypole was the trunk of a straight young oak-tree. It was used year after year, and betweentime it was kept on brackets under the thatched eaves of the church hall. About a week before May Day it had been taken down, painted and fitted into its foundation stone. The long many-coloured ribbons used in maypole dancing were fastened to its top before it was pulled upright, for when erect it stood more than twenty feet tall.

Throughout the week the school children had been practising maypole dancing, so now they were quite expert. The band provided the music as each child held the end of a ribbon and danced in a circle around the maypole. At a signal the dancers started weaving in and out, passing each other first on one side and then another. The ribbons wound themselves tightly around the pole, starting at the top, until, at the end, the pole was covered from top to bottom with criss-crossed ribbons and the children were gathered in a tight circle at the foot. Then, at another signal, they started to unwind again, ending the dance as they had begun.

Maypole dancing is energetic, too, so when the performance ended the children rested while the Morris dancers took over. Then, as preparations for the feast were still going on, the children, including Clara, began another dance around the maypole.

They were just starting the movement to wrap the ribbons around the maypole when someone shouted,

'Look out! Cattle!'

Before anyone had a chance to do anything a herd of wild young cattle stampeded across the green and into the crowd of dancers and onlookers. For the next few minutes there was pandemonium. Men shouted, women screamed, people tripped and went sprawling on the grass, dogs barked enthusiastically, the band stopped playing and the bandsmen joined in the shouting. One of the animals blundered against the guy-ropes holding the maypole up. For a moment the maypole swayed, then it came crashing to the ground, ribbons flying everywhere. Fortunately no-one was immediately underneath. Clara, clambering to her feet after tumbling headlong and burying her nose in the grass, found a yellow ribbon wrapped around her head and shoulders. The cattle, too, were galloping away, festooned in ribbons. One of them had the May Queen's crown dangling from its horns.

It took a few minutes for everyone to recover from the shock. Happily no-one was hurt, though dresses and costumes had been

damaged and stained with grass marks. Being village folk, however, the people were used to cattle and sheep escaping from their fields and soon they were laughing about it all.

But where did the cattle come from? It was soon established that they belonged to Clara's father. They were the heifers which had been turned out to grass earlier in the afternoon. And how they had managed to escape was soon explained. They had come through Mr Purdle's orchard, both gates of which were open. He had forgotten to shut them.

'I wonder where my crown is?' said Gwen Pothecary mournfully.

A search party went looking for the cattle. They soon found them in Mr Purdle's garden, eating his cabbages. He had forgotten to shut his garden gate, too.

'Serve him right,' was everybody's opinion.

4 *May*

Beating the Bounds

Today Clara was glad she was not a boy.

Usually she envied her brother Giles, who was twelve and two years older than herself, but she would have hated to be Giles on Rogation Day. It didn't seem a bit fair that he should be beaten, especially as he hadn't done anything wrong. (Still, the day had ended well, with all that excitement and Mr Purdle's downfall. She had enjoyed that.)

Rogation Day was a Sunday, of course. After morning church they had dinner and then met other villagers on the green. There were forty or fifty of them, all people whom Clara knew, including her best friends, Sarah and Emmie. They had made up their minds to walk together as soon as the procession started. Giles and his friends were there, too, but each of them stood with his parents and didn't seem to want to talk. They knew what was in store for them.

The bells were ringing as the vicar came stumping down the path from the Vicarage, his heavy boots lifting the hem of his white surplice as he walked. The flag with the red cross on the white ground, the flag of England, still fluttered from the church tower, where it had been hoisted on St George's Day, 23 April. It had a double significance, for the church was dedicated to St George, and Billy Shammick was carrying the parish banner, all golden with green tassels and embroidered with *Cowbourne St George* in red.

When the last echoes of the bells had died away, old Peter tried a chord on his fiddle, and they all sang the hymn, 'All people that on earth do dwell'. Eli and James and several other men had brought their musical instruments as well, some cornets and trumpets and some violins, but Little Tom had left his drum at home, it being too heavy to be carried on the long march. Several of the old folk, whose legs were too feeble to take them so far, leaned over their garden gates and joined in the singing, and the chaffinches, blackbirds, thrushes and other birds also helped, though they didn't know when to stop and kept calling all through the vicar's prayer.

Then the vicar, Reverend Marcus Latimer, gave the little speech which he always delivered on Rogation Day. He reminded his congregation of the unity of the parish, with the church as its centre. He likened them to a flock of sheep, with himself as the shepherd. He commended their work in the fields and gardens and told them that they were now going to ask God's blessing on all they had been doing, by ploughing, sowing and weeding, to produce a harvest.

'And now, as our ancestors have done for many centuries,' he went on, 'we are going to walk around the boundaries of this parish which is our home, marking its limits and reminding ourselves of the extent of the heritage which God has given us, to cultivate for our own wellbeing and His glory.'

When he had finished, he stood with his face towards the lane that went westwards, towards the hill, and the people formed in procession behind him. Billy Shammick walked by his side, and after them came the band, playing marching hymns. Old Joshua Mendip, the carpenter, who had a great, deep voice, sang some of the verses he could remember, and some of the other people joined in, but mostly they saved their breath, for they knew they had a long way to go. At the tail end of the procession three young men pushed the covered hand-cart that on other days Walter Vernditch, the baker, used for delivering his loaves of bread. Today it was filled not only with bread but with cakes, pies, cheese and casks of cider. It was so heavy that all three were needed to keep it moving. Several dogs decided to come along, too, as did Major, the piebald pony who was grazing on the green.

'It's a pity we can't get him to pull this cart,' said one of the young men, but they had no harness for him, and the cart was not fitted with shafts.

At the school, which stood at the end of the village, they stopped for another hymn and a prayer, and then continued along the rutted, pot-holed road between the hedges that led to the clump of trees on the very summit of Chardown Hill.

The storms of the past two days had fled away, and the sun beamed down as warmly as it should do in mid-May, drying up the mud and calling on all the spring flowers to open their petals. The hedge-banks were as gay as a bride's-maid's posy with pink campions, bluebells, lace-like cow-parsley, cuckoo-flowers, golden dandelions and dozens of other flowers, all of which Clara knew by name, being a country girl. Henry Gray's orchard, which they passed, was foaming with pink and white blossom, as though it had been whipped up into a froth. A cuckoo was calling from one of the apple trees but flew away as the procession approached.

'There it is! The cuckoo!' exclaimed the children. They always referred to it as *the* cuckoo, never as *a* cuckoo, because most of them thought there was only one cuckoo in the world, though Clara was sure that, once, she had heard two of them calling together.

When they began to climb the winding hill the procession soon started to tail off. One by one the musical instruments ceased playing, and the hymns came to an end. Old Mrs Enticott, who had insisted on coming along, although she was nearly eighty, had to sit on a stone heap for a few minutes, to get her breath back, and Clara's mother and another woman sat with her. While they were resting Clara and the girls peered into the hedges, looking for birds' nests. They soon found one—a hedge-sparrow's, with four smooth, blue-green eggs. Clara wanted to show it to Giles, but none of the boys was in a mood for birds'-nesting today. The men with the hand-cart were finding the work so hard that several others moved back to help them.

'The cart would be lighter if we drank some of that cider,' complained one of the young men, hopefully, but Clara's grandfather, who was one of the important men of the village, was stern.

'Not until we get to the top of the hill,' he insisted.

At last they were there, in a round clump of beech trees that was surrounded by a very old earthwork built by prehistoric men. The bright green leaves of the beeches had just opened, forming a canopy overhead through which the sunbeams cast dappled shadows on the dead, brown leaves of last year. Not as many flowers grew under the trees as in the hedge-banks, but there were drifts of woodruff, with tiny, white, star-like flowers. Clara and the girls hastened to pick handfuls, for if you put it in the linen drawer it made the clothes smell fresh and fragrant.

In the middle of the wood, on the highest point of the hill, was a low heap of stones. Here Joshua Mendip stood and read a chapter from the Bible about boundary stones and curses on anyone who moves them. They sang a hymn, and the vicar read a prayer. Then he announced,

'Here we stand at the point where our parish of Cowbourne St George meets the parishes of Mellersley and Tackham. Let this spot be held in good remembrance for ever.'

'Amen,' said everyone, and Mr Purdle, the sexton, grabbed Stephen Harrasmith, who was one of Giles's best friends, and pushed him forward, face-down, on the heap of stones. Two men stepped forward to hold Stephen there, while the sexton beat him hard with a flat stick he had brought along. Some of the other men had cut hazel rods out of the hedges as they came along, and they, too, got in a shrewd blow or two on Stephen's bottom. Stephen wriggled and yelled, but he couldn't get free, and before they had finished tears were running down his face.

'Aoww! Oooo! Don't! No, stop it!' he shouted, but they only beat him harder.

Clara hated to see him hurt like that.

'It's not fair!' she told her mother. 'He hasn't done anything!'

'No, but it is a custom,' replied her mother. 'It happened to your father and grandfather, when they were boys, and now it is happening to Stephen and Giles. You see, it is very important for the people of our village to remember where the boundaries are, so we walk around them every year, on Rogation Day, and stop for a hymn and a prayer at every junction. Then the boys are beaten so that they will always remember. Your grandfather will remember, even now, that he was walloped here nearly seventy years ago.'

Clara thought they ought to be able to remember without being beaten like that, but now it was over and refreshments were being handed round so she dashed forward to get her share. She noticed that people were making a fuss of Stephen now and that he was given a special iced cake.

'I think he would remember just as well if he got the iced cake without the beating,' thought Clara.

They left Chardown Hill by another route, descending into the Oxbrook valley and crossing the marsh by the causeway. They came to cross-roads overshadowed by a great spreading oak tree, like an umbrella. The Gospel Oak, it was called, because this was another of the Rogation-tide stops where the Gospel was read. Once again, after the reading, a hymn was sung and a prayer said, and then a boy was stood against the oak and beaten. This time it was Jim Mettish, and once again Mr Purdle, who didn't like boys at all, took the lead in making his bottom sting. Clara noticed the grin on his face as he brought down the stick hard.

'I'd like to wallop him with stinging-nettles,' she thought.

On they went, through the woods, where the next stopping-point was a narrow stone bridge over a tiny stream. Here Dickie Vell was the victim, and his yells set all the pheasants in the woods calling.

'Go easy on him,' said Clara's grandfather. 'You don't need to lay it on too hard.'

But Mr Purdle was enjoying himself and took no notice.

They had now walked several miles in a huge semi-circle around the village. As they approached the next station, which was an upright stone just inside a meadow, they could see the houses not very far away across the fields. The handcart was becoming lighter, as the refreshments were consumed, but the men who were pushing it were growing more and more tired, so it seemed just as heavy.

'Let's call it a day,' muttered one of them. But they knew they had a few miles still to go, to complete the circle.

The Bible was read by Clara's Uncle Bart, the hymn was sung and the prayer given. Now it was Giles's turn. Mr Purdle reached out for him, but at the last moment Giles's nerve failed. He ducked under Mr Purdle's arm, dodged like a frightened rabbit, and raced away across the meadow towards home, the roof of which he could see just above the trees.

'Hey! Hey! Come back, you young devil!' shouted Mr Purdle, forgetting that the vicar was present, and starting to chase after Giles. Several of the other men joined in, though the hand-cart team was on Giles's side.

'Go it, young 'un,' they shouted.

'He's got the right idea,' said one. 'I wouldn't mind going home, too.'

'Let's have a mug of cider while we're waiting,' said another, and they all thought that was the best idea of all.

'Run, Giles! Run!' screamed Clara, and the other girls shouted, too, and clapped their hands in excitement. The vicar stood gazing at the chase and not knowing what to do, but out of the corner of her eye Clara saw her grandfather standing like a tree buffeted by the wind, shaking with laughter.

The running figures grew more distant. Giles was in the lead, still running strongly, though stumbling now and again in boggy places and over ant-hills. Then came Mr Purdle, brandishing his big stick and still shouting threats. The rest were strung out behind, like huntsmen after a fox.

Then, suddenly, Clara noticed a change. The men were all running the other way. They were coming back to the meadow gate where everyone else was waiting. All except Giles, who had swerved to the right and had nearly reached a gap in the hedge. Now in the middle of the field, tossing his head and moving at a fast trot, was Granddad's huge, shaggy, long-horned bull. He was ignoring Giles, who, in any case, was now nearly safely through the hedge, and was giving

his full attention to all these cheeky men who were daring to invade his domain.

Everyone in the waiting party made haste to move out of the meadow and fasten the gate, except Clara's grandfather who said to the vicar,

'I'd forgotten the bull was in this field. I'd better go and stop him.'

The men who had been the last to start the chase were now arriving back, panting and eager to be on the safe side of the gate. The others would soon be there. But Mr Purdle, of course, having been so eager to start chasing Giles, was last.

'Help! Help!' he called.

Grand-dad walked towards him to help, but he was old and stiff and couldn't move very fast, and now the bull, with his head down, was advancing at a gallop. Mr Purdle threw away his big stick and tried to run faster, but the bull, catching him on the edge of a ditch, cannoned into his rear with the force of a shunting railway engine, and lifted him high into the air.

Everyone watched in fascination as Mr Purdle soared above the meadow, arms and legs threshing about, and finally came down in a watery bog, amid clumps of golden marsh marigold, water-mint, brambles and a flourishing plot of nettles. His screams could be heard down in the village, and everyone who had not joined the Rogationtide procession must have wondered what in the world was happening.

Once the bull had tossed his victim he seemed satisfied. He stopped running and stood swishing his tail from side to side, preparing to chase Mr Purdle again if he should emerge from the water. When Grand-dad came near and began talking to him he recognized a voice he knew and obediently moved away when Grand-dad scolded him. Clara's father and Eli and James, who had also had dealings with the bull, went across to help Mr Purdle out of the bramble and nettle patch, while Grand-dad stood on guard; but all the other people stayed on the safe side of the gate.

'I think that perhaps we had better let that do for today,' suggested the vicar, as they came back, helping the dripping, muddy, grumbling Mr Purdle between them.

'It's starting to rain, anyway,' Clara's Uncle Bart pointed out.

'Have you got room for Mr Purdle on the hand-cart?' asked someone.

'No,' replied one of the team.

'Anyhow, he can't sit down!' said another, laughing. Mr Purdle started using such bad language that one of the men put a hand over his mouth, to stop him before the vicar heard.

'There's one thing,' remarked Clara's mother, as they hurried home through the rain-drops, 'everyone will always remember this Rogation Day and the boundary mark of the Standing Stone, even although Giles wasn't beaten there.'

Clara thought so, too.

5 *June*

Midsummer Fleeces and Festivals

Clara's father had had unwelcome news at dinner-time, brought by a boy from a village four miles away.

'What a nuisance!' he explained. 'The shearing gang can't be here until the third week of June.'

'Perhaps we could do the shearing ourselves?' Uncle George suggested.

'It's possible,' said Clara's father, pondering.

'Leave it,' was Grand-dad's opinion. 'Be thankful it's happened like this. The weather looks set fine and the grass is ready for cutting. Let's get on with the haymaking and be thankful that we don't have to interrupt it to shear the sheep.'

'That's one way of looking at it,' her father agreed.

'But it's so hot for the sheep with their winter fleeces on,' objected Uncle George. 'They'll get heat-stroke.'

'Put them on the downs on top of the hill,' Grand-dad advised. 'It's always breezy up there. They'll be cool enough.'

So it was decided, and for the next two or three weeks everyone on the farm was busy hay-making. Some of the men mowed the grass with scythes, and some turned it with rakes and forks. After leaving it to dry for about a week, turning it every day, it was perfectly 'made' and ready to be carted to the rickyard. There it was stored in ricks to feed the cattle, sheep and horses in winter.

Clara and Giles were at school during the day, but in the evenings they were expected to help in the hayfields. Usually they had to help to turn the hay, but when carting was in progress they sometimes had to lead the horses. Most of the women, except Clara's mother and grandmother, who had plenty to keep them busy in the kitchen, were also at work in the hayfields. When they came home from school Clara and Giles used to harness Dandy, the donkey, load the donkey-cart with cans of hot tea, stone jars of cider and baskets of food, and take them to the fields for the haymakers. There they also sat on the ground, amid piles of fragrant hay, and enjoyed a picnic. These country children had no school homework, but they had to work quite late in the evenings, and when they went to bed they fell asleep as soon as their heads touched their pillows. But it was fun and Clara and Giles loved haymaking.

One Saturday, when about two-thirds of the haymaking was finished, Clara's father, Uncle Jonah and Uncle Luther decided to take the sheep to the river for washing. They chose a Saturday so that Clara and Giles could help.

'That means that we won't have to take so many people away from the hay,' said Clara's father. 'Those two children are quite capable of helping to drive sheep.'

The nearest river was three miles away from the downs where the sheep were grazing. The men, and Clara and Giles, set off immediately after breakfast, with stout sticks to help them walking and with satchels of food and drink on their backs. Toby, of course, was there, and one other sheepdog, a shaggy grey-and-white one named Jess, who belonged to Uncle Jonah. When they arrived at the downs Uncle Jonah sent the dogs to round up the sheep, a job which would have taken the men an hour or two but which they managed in about ten minutes.

Once they had left the unfenced downs they travelled along lanes, mostly between hedges, so the sheep had few opportunities for straying. Clara and Giles had to run on ahead and shut any gates which had been left open.

'Keep back,' shouted Clara breathlessly, as the sheep pressed forward, breaking at times into a trot. 'Don't go so fast!'

Then, just as she thought she couldn't run any farther, the sheep would find an open, grassy place and stop to graze.

In a meadow by the river was an arrangement of hurdle-pens and hatches known as a 'sheepwash'. It belonged to a farmer named Mr Hillier, who kept it in repair and charged other farmers for using it.

All the sheep were first penned in a large meadow a little way upstream. From there they were guided in batches to a smaller enclosure of hurdles on the edge of a channel leading off the main river. Clara's father adjusted a hatch so that the water on the other side of it was deep. He and Uncle Jonah took up stations on either side of this deep pool. Each was armed with a pole which had a flat board nailed at right angles at the end. Uncle Luther guided the sheep to the edge of the pool and pushed them in one by one. As they floundered about frantically the two men scrubbed them with the boards. After a bit the sheep drifted downstream to where the water was shallower and where they could scramble up the bank, shaking themselves like dogs.

'This'll wash all the dirt and hayseeds out of their fleeces,' Clara's father remarked as they washed the first one. 'They get very dirty during the winter, and we must have good clean fleeces to sell.'

Clara felt a bit sorry for the sheep at the beginning and was afraid that some of them might drown. But none of them did and they certainly looked better for their dip. Those which had been washed stood contentedly sunning themselves or nibbling grass, completely ignoring the baaing and splashing of those still having their bath. Toby and Jess jumped into the pool with the sheep several times for the sheer joy of it. The men obligingly scrubbed their backs.

Washing about two hundred ewes took a long time but at last the task was finished. Clara, Giles and the men sat on the river bank and ate their lunch. The sun burned so hot on their backs that Giles thought it would be good to go bathing like the sheep.

'Better not,' said his father. 'The water's colder than you think, and, besides, you haven't got a towel.'

So they took off their shoes and stockings and let their feet dangle in the gently-flowing water while they shared bread and cheese with Toby and Jess. All around them in the meadows corncrakes were giving their harsh calls which sounded as though they were trying to repeat their name. (Corncrakes are brown birds, about as big as moorhens, which were once common in English meadows but are now seldom heard.) Skylarks were singing overhead, and once Giles pointed out what appeared to Clara to be a bright yellow butterfly flitting over the river a hundred yards downstream.

'It's a yellow wagtail!' he exclaimed. Yellow wagtails are summer visitors, like swallows, but only in small numbers. To see one is quite an event.

When they all arrived home the children were very tired, but after a good tea they still felt energetic enough to help with the haymaking for an hour or two.

'Many hands make light work,' their father quoted, by way of encouragement. 'It's been a wonderful haymaking so far, but we must get all the hay safe, if we can, before the weather changes.'

They just managed it. On the afternoon after the last load of hay was carted to the rickyard the air became hotter and more sultry than ever and the sun changed to a coppery colour. Clara felt so tired that she went up to her bedroom and lay on the bed, where, presently, two of the cats came to join her.

When she came downstairs the light seemed to be fading. Looking out of the window she could see an ominous blackness blotting out the horizon to the south. The outline of the hills was visible only when quivering flashes of lightning illuminated it.

'Oh, we're going to have a thunderstorm!' she exclaimed.

'Too true we are,' her granny agreed, 'and a heavy one. The animals know it.'

Clara looked around and saw that every one of the cats, except the two which were still curled up on her bed, were now in the living room, most of them under the table. Toby was there, too, hiding behind his master's armchair.

'They can hear thunder a long time before we can,' said Granny.

At last Clara and even her granny, who was growing deaf, could hear it. The lightning was now playing vividly and illuminating the whole sky, which otherwise was sooty black.

'Well, everything's safely under cover, I think,' said Clara's father, as he and the other men came in. 'We must hope nothing gets struck by lightning. What a good thing we've finished haymaking.'

Then, almost as he was speaking, the rain came sweeping and splashing across the meadows and hitting the windows like a cascade of gravel. A flash of lightning made the room as bright as noonday, and almost immediately a tremendous explosion of thunder seemed to shake the house. Toby took refuge, trembling, between his master's legs, while two more of the cats fled upstairs.

The storm continued all the evening. When Clara went to bed at nine o'clock rain was still pouring down, although the thunder and lightning were receding. As she was dropping off to sleep she could see the frequent flickering of lightning along the line of the northern hills, but the monotonous drumming of the rain on the window-panes was soothing and she was soon fast asleep.

For more than a week after that it rained most days. Some of the other farmers who hadn't finished their haymaking had their fields of hay saturated and spoiled. And word came that there would be a further delay before the sheep shearing could begin; the farm where the shearers had been working had been flooded.

'Perhaps it's just as well,' said Clara's grand-dad, looking on the bright side as always. 'The weather's a lot colder since the thunder. It's a good thing the sheep didn't lose their coats just before that storm, or they'd have been likely to catch a chill.'

'It looks to me as though sheep-shearing will about coincide with midsummer,' said Granny. 'We shall be able to have both the feasts together.'

The shearers arrived at mid-day, two days before Midsummer. There were four of them.

'We've split the gang because we're all behindhand with our work,' the leader explained, 'and we always get plenty of help on this farm. Four of us have gone on to Higher Barn Farm.'

The shearing gang contracted to shear most of the sheep within

eight or ten miles of the village. The men were expert shearers, and could each shear thirty to fifty sheep a day. Some of them lived in the same village as Clara, the others in neighbouring villages. Their leader was Luke Theaker, who had a small farm about a mile along the road and whose daughter, Minnie, went to Clara's school.

'So you'll be finishing here tomorrow, and tomorrow is Midsummer Eve,' Clara's mother said to Luke Theaker. 'You'd better tell your wife to come along and help with the preparations.'

The next day everyone was exceptionally busy. The sheep had been fetched from the pastures and were penned in the great barn. The shearers, which included Uncle Jonah besides the four visiting experts, were lined up along the threshing floor. As though at a signal, they dived into the pen of sheep, and each extracted an animal which he dragged, struggling to the floor. There he upended it, sitting the sheep on its rump and placing his left arm across its neck, and began clipping with the shears. These, of course, were hand shears, not the electric models now used.

With deft sweeps of the arm the shearers expertly removed the fleeces in one piece. The sheep, realizing that struggling was useless, soon gave up and sat there docilely. Uncle George, standing nearby, had a pot of Stockholm tar and a brush, to dab on any sheep that got nicked, as disinfectant, but he had to treat very few. When the fleece fell to the floor the sheep, released, went bounding away, baaing loudly, to join its shorn comrades. They were allowed to escape from the barn into the sunlit meadow, where they jumped about like young lambs, pleased to be rid of their heavy overcoats. Clara's father, Uncle Bart and Eli were in the meantime gathering up the fleeces, tying them into bundles and packing them into enormous sacks known as wool-sacks.

In the orchard behind the farm old Peter was also busy with a sheep, but this was a dead one. He was roasting it for the evening feast.

'Having a shearing feast always seems a nice neighbourly thing to do,' said Clara's granny. 'It's even better, though, when we can combine it with Midsummer celebrations.'

Mrs Theaker and the wives of the other shearers had arrived and were busily helping Clara's mother, grandmother and aunts to prepare the food. The first vegetables of the season were ripening in the garden, so there were bucketfuls of new potatoes to be scraped, gallons of peas and broad beans to be shelled and cabbages to be sliced. Clara's granny was endlessly stirring a stock-pot which hung over the hearth fire in the living-room, a fire which had to be lit, although the weather was warm, because there was not room for everything on the kitchen stove. Clara loved the stock-pot and the appetising scents that rose from it. She was especially pleased to see her granny pouring pints of pearl barley, which she loved, into the mixture.

Then something more exciting arrived. Mr Harding, the nurseryman from Bournechurch, drove into the yard with his pony and trap and started unloading baskets and baskets of ripe strawberries.

'Ooo! Strawberries!' breathed Clara, her eyes sparkling.

'Fingers away!' warned her mother.

'Oh well, just one or two,' she added, relenting. 'That's one advantage in having the shearing feast late. The strawberries have had time to ripen.'

When the last sheep had been shorn and had bounded, bleating, into the meadow the men came in to tidy themselves before supper, which they ate outdoors. Trestle-tables had been laid under the apple-trees in the orchard, not far from where the sheep was roasting. After they had sung a grace, Clara's father carved slices of meat, her mother served potatoes, Aunt Martha doled out dumplings, some of the other women supplied helpings of other vegetables, Aunt Tillie handed around newly-baked bread rolls, and Granny ladled out gravy from the stock-pot. It was lovely, sitting there in the shade of the trees with all her family and friends. Not forgetting Toby. He had attached himself to Clara and was sitting on the grass with his head against her knee, waiting for whatever she cared to give him. Clara found he especially liked bits of bread soaked in gravy.

After the first course came the strawberries, which Clara's mother had mashed in milk. Each person had a basinful, into which they dropped brown bread broken into small pieces. That is the best way of eating strawberries, as everybody present knew. Jugs of fresh cream were on the table for anyone who wanted it.

Swifts wheeled overhead, a cuckoo was still calling, and a white owl drifted through the orchard, compelled to hunt mice by daylight now that the nights were so short. Clara's father and some of the other men had lit their pipes. Clara went and sat on his knee, partly because she liked the smell of his tobacco and partly because the smoke drove away the midges, which were beginning to bite as twilight approached.

'Time to light the bonfire, eh, moppet?' said her father, and Clara nodded in agreement.

Old Peter had been trimming hedges for fuel for the bonfire over the past few weeks, but in the thunderstorm a dead hawthorn tree had been blown down and this, added to the heap that Peter had collected, made an impressive pyre. Forkfuls of dry straw had been

pressed between the bushes to get the fire started. Clara's father lit them, and soon the flames were leaping high.

'Come and dance around it, Clara,' called her young Uncle George. She joined hands with him and Aunt Miriam, then Minnie Theaker and Giles and more children and young people joined in and soon they had enough to encircle the fire.

'The other way!' Granny called, 'the other way!' as they started to dance. When they stopped she explained,

'You must always dance clockwise around a Midsummer fire,' she explained. 'Otherwise you will be inviting bad luck, not good.'

When the fire died down sufficiently some of the boys and older girls leaped through the flickering flames, sending up a little cloud of hot ashes as they landed on the other side. That was for good luck, too.

Clara's grand-dad told her that dancing around the fire was supposed to represent the circle of the sun as it rode across the heavens from east to west. Jumping through the flames was supposed to be a safeguard against illness. In the old days, he said, cattle and horses used to be driven through the embers of the Midsummer fire for the same reason.

'But I don't believe it did them any good,' he grinned.

'By rights I ought to have the Hobby-Horse here, to liven things up,' lamented Uncle George. 'But the vicar has locked it in the vestry and he won't let me have the key!'

Back in the house Clara's aunts showed her some of the Midsummer spells. They had decorated the windowsills with golden St John's-wort and had hung bunches of it over the back and front doors to keep evil spirits at bay, they said, though they laughed as though they didn't believe it. They placed sprigs of orpine (which is a fleshy plant that bears a pink flower at Midsummer) on plates, two on each plate, to represent each aunt and her husband or, in the case of Aunt Martha, the unknown man whom she hoped she might marry one day. In the morning if the two stems were bending towards each other their married life would be happy; if they were turning away from each other, domestic storms lay ahead. Aunt Miriam showed her some little lumps of a black substance which she called 'coals' and which she had dug from the roots of a roadside plant called mugwort. She urged Aunt Martha to place it under her pillow at night, and she would be sure to dream of her future husband. Aunt Martha blushed and said she would certainly do no such thing, but she took the 'coals' and put them in her pocket. Aunt Miriam also had a rose which she had picked that evening.

'They say that a rose picked at Midsummer will remain fresh till Christmas,' she said. 'Well, we shall see.'

Granny came into the room.

'Are you girls thinking of staying up all night?' she enquired.

'Good heavens! it's past eleven o'clock!' exclaimed Aunt Tillie, looking at the clock. 'I had no idea. It's hardly dark.'

'Well, after all, it is one of the longest days,' Granny said. 'But when I was a girl people did stay up all night on Midsummer Eve. They were afraid to go to sleep because it was said that on that night your spirit went wandering and it might not be able to find its way back to your body.'

Clara thought about this and wondered whether it would be safe to go to bed. When, a little later, she asked Giles he was eager to try.

'It would be fun to go wandering about at night without anyone being able to see you,' he said.

'If you want to do that there's a better way,' said Uncle George, who overheard him. 'You gather fern seed on a pewter plate at midnight and it makes you invisible.'

'Honest?' asked Giles. 'Shall we try it? I'm not tired.'

'Nor am I,' declared Clara.

'There's a lot of ferns under the trees at the edge of the churchyard,' said Uncle George. 'We can but try.'

The three set out, Uncle George carrying a candle-powered lantern and wearing over his other clothes the white smock he had been using all day, for the evening was growing chilly. Giles carried a pewter plate and Clara kept hold of Uncle George's arm. It was now almost dark, though the stars seemed very brilliant.

When they got to the churchyard, which took them about a quarter of an hour, they picked their way among the tombstones to the far side, where the enclosure bordered the forest.

'They should be just over here,' said Uncle George in a low voice.

'Ssh. Hide the light! There's someone over there!'

Uncle George quickly thrust the lantern under his smock, and all three stood stock still, holding their breath. A dim figure was stumbling among the tombstones, moving towards them. Presently it found one, shaped like a table, under a dark yew tree and sat down on it. A flicker of light showed that it was lighting a pipe.

'I know who it is,' Giles whispered. 'It's Mr Purdle, the sexton.'

'And I know why he's here,' Uncle George whispered back. 'I've heard he does this but I hardly believed it. It's said that on Midsummer Eve at midnight the souls of all those in the village who are going to die in the coming year may be seen passing into the church. Old Purdle comes to watch for them, so that he'll know how many graves he'll have to dig. I'll bet he works out how much money he'll get in fees, too.'

They stood silent for a few moments.

'What shall we do?' asked Clara. 'If we start moving about with the lantern he'll see us.'

'Yes,' agreed Uncle George.

'I know what!' he exclaimed suddenly. 'Let's give him a fright. You stay here and watch. Hold the lantern under your coat, Giles.'

Giles did so and Clara clutched his arm. Uncle George vanished.

Presently they heard a wild, unearthly shriek from the darkness near the yew tree. Then a weird, hollow voice called,

'IT'S YOU I'LL BE COMING FOR . . . IT'S YOU . . . AND BEFORE VERY LONG.'

Although she knew it was Uncle George Clara felt shivers run up and down her spine, and she held Giles' arm tighter. Especially when a ghostly white figure, like a huge balloon, appeared and started drifting across the churchyard.

Of course, that was Uncle George, too, his smock spread over his outstretched arms, but Giles' old enemy, Mr Purdle, didn't know that. They saw him suddenly emerge from the gloom of the yew tree and rush helter-skelter towards the road, stumbling over graves as he fled. His arms were thrown out in front of him, and his glowing pipe had fallen on the grass. He was too frightened even to shout.

Giles was so excited he could hardly keep quiet.

'Jolly good, Uncle George!' he muttered, trying hard not to raise his voice. 'Jolly good! That'll teach him!'

Then he stopped, and his words died in a gurgle. The white form approaching them was not Uncle George in his white smock but . . . SOMETHING ELSE! A big shapeless white blur, steadily advancing towards them!

It was only a white cow which had strayed into the churchyard, but they didn't stay to discover that. Forgetting Uncle George completely, they covered the homeward journey in not much more than five minutes. Clara only just managed to keep up with Giles. When they had paused outside the farmhouse door long enough to recover their breath they went in, said a quick goodnight to their parents and ran upstairs to bed. They had had enough of midnight expeditions on Midsummer Eve.

6 *August*
The Festival of the Little Loaves

'You must always sing when you are picking strawberries,' Clara's grandfather told her, his eyes twinkling.

Clara, who liked singing, thought that was a happy idea, until she realized that when she was singing she couldn't eat any strawberries! But her grandfather was only joking. She was allowed to eat as many as she liked, though, curiously, after a dozen or two she didn't want any more.

But now, in the last week of July, the strawberry season was almost over. There were still plenty of the little wild strawberries, which taste so much sweeter than the big luscious ones in the garden, but the latter had all been picked or eaten by birds. Now Clara had to spend hours helping to pick raspberries, gooseberries, currants and peas.

The end of the school term meant for Clara simply a change of work. It was pleasant to be outdoors instead of sitting on a hard seat in the classroom, but summer was harvest time, not holiday time. The church school closed for six weeks simply to allow the children to stay at home to help with the harvest. Everything ripened in summer and had to be gathered for use in the coming winter. There was so much to do that even children had to help. When Clara was not picking fruit she sat on a stool in the cobbled courtyard outside the kitchen door, shelling peas or snipping the tops and tails (dead petals and stems) off gooseberries or stripping currants from their stems. Nearby old Peter turned the butter churn and complained endlessly about the reluctance of the cream to change into butter in hot weather. Wisps of scented steam curling out of the kitchen window were a reminder that indoors Clara's mother and grandmother were making jam. It was pleasant enough, sitting there in the warm sunshine, but Clara wished there was not quite as much work to do. She would have liked to go down to the brook and lie on the soft grass under the willow-trees, watching the dragon-flies. She knew, though, that this was only the beginning. Very soon the corn harvest would start, and then everyone would be even busier.

She envied the cats, stretched out lazily on the paving-stones. There were always plenty of cats on the farm, and at present six kittens, a month or two old, were lying half-asleep on and around their mothers and aunts, while old Samkin, the big black-and-white tom, lolled, with eyes half-closed, on an upturned wheelbarrow. At nights the adult cats went hunting for mice and voles in the long grass, but all day long they did nothing but bask in the sun, except when Clara's mother brought out food for them.

Even when Toby, the big, shaggy sheep-dog, came bounding into the yard the cats did not stir. Cats and dogs are usually good friends when they have been brought up together, and Toby had lived on the farm since he was a puppy. But although the cats took no notice of him, Clara did. Toby was like her father's shadow. He followed her father everywhere, unless he was tied up, and then he howled and barked until he was let loose. So Clara put down the half-filled bowl of shelled peas and made ready to greet her father as he came striding through the yard gate.

'Hello there, moppet,' said her father, 'ready for harvest?'

'Are we going to start today?' asked Clara.

'This very afternoon,' her father assured her and her mother who had come to the kitchen door. 'I've just taken a look at the wheat in

Beech Acres and it's fit to cut straight away.'

'May I bring up the tea for the men?' Clara enquired, thinking of her usual harvest task.

'I dare say,' said her father.

Well, being tea-lady to the harvesters was a change from sitting in the back yard, shelling peas. In the middle of the afternoon Clara took Dandy's bridle to the orchard where the donkey was grazing, led her back to the cart-shed and harnessed her to the cart which the carpenter and blacksmith had made specially for her. Old Peter pottered about, making sure the harness was secure, though Clara thought that was quite unnecessary. Her mother came out carrying a heavy bucket covered with a lid and wrapped in sacking, to prevent the hot tea from cooling. Aunt Martha followed, pushing a trolley with a cask of cider, for the men who preferred cider to tea. Then came her grandmother, with a big basket of bread, cheese, cake and apples on her arm.

When all the provisions had been stacked in the donkey cart and the tea bucket wedged in so that the tea would not slop over, Clara was ready to start.

'You'll have to walk and lead her,' said Aunt Martha, who was fussy and thought that children couldn't think things out for themselves.

'I know,' said Clara. Apart from the facts that the lane to Beech Acres was all uphill and the cart was heavily laden, Dandy didn't like going away from home. It would be different when they were coming back to the farm, downhill all the way.

So Dandy plodded slowly up the winding lane, between the tall, brambly hedges where the rose-hips were turning red and late blossoms of the sweet-scented honeysuckle were still blooming. The season of singing birds was nearly past, but a solitary cock yellow hammer, his plumage as bright as a canary's, was still wheezing out his monotonous song from the top of a thorn hedge. 'A little bit of bread and no cheese' was what Clara had been told he was trying to say. It sounded a bit like that. She repeated the words and was reminded that the wild cheeses were probably ripe. They were the ripening fruits of the mallow, a sprawling plant with bright pink

flowers and, searching among the plants on the hedge-banks, she found plenty. When the calyces were stripped off, these little fruits were round and flat, like miniature cheeses. Clara nibbled them. They had a pleasant taste but more like nuts than cheese, and she decided that they must have been given their name because of their shape, not their flavour.

A little farther on she found a clump of bushes of very early blackberries and some straggling brambles bearing the tiny powdery-blue variety of blackberries which Clara called dewberries. Just before she arrived at the harvest field she knew she would find a thicket of wild raspberries, which would now be ripe for eating. Clara sampled them all. When all the wild fruits and berries started to ripen it was a sure sign that harvest was ready, she thought.

On a piece of waste ground near the corner of the wheat-field the men had gathered. Her father was talking to Uncle Bart and Uncle Luther, while Eli and James sharpened their scythes with blue whetstones, making a cutting, scissory noise, and Uncle George was romping with his dog Scamp. Toby, the dog, gave a warning bark. Then, recognizing Clara, he came bounding to meet her.

'Hooray! Tea!' shouted Uncle George, jumping up and following Toby.

'Not so fast,' her father told him. 'We must make a start first.'

They unloaded the cart and placed the food and drink on the ground under a shady sycamore tree. Eli tied Dandy to a stake nearby. Then her father made all the men line up, ready to begin cutting the stalks of wheat with their scythes. At a word from him they all bent their backs and began to work, swinging their scythes with a smooth, easy motion. Swish, swish, said the scythes, and the tall stalks toppled over and lay in neat lines on the ground. Clara gathered up an armful or two and placed them ready to be tied into bundles, as she had seen her mother and aunts do.

After a short time her father said 'That's enough.' So they all stopped mowing and tied the wheat stalks into sheaves, using twisted straw for string. They had enough for twelve large sheaves.

'Now we'll have a bite before we start in earnest,' said her father, 'then Clara and I will take these sheaves down to the farm.'

Clara enjoyed sitting under the sycamore tree, having tea with the men. The dogs sat around looking longingly at each mouthful, saliva dripping from their mouths, and every now and then they were rewarded with a titbit. Uncle George found a fat orange spider to tease Clara with, but fortunately Clara wasn't scared of spiders and she thought this one rather beautiful. All around them blue, brown and white butterflies danced from flower to flower, and grasshoppers sang their reedy song, as they do in warm weather.

It came to an end too quickly, though Clara knew it would be the first picnic of many. The tea bucket and the cider cask were left under the hedge for the men to use again later on, but the empty basket was returned to the cart. On top of it the twelve sheaves were packed. Then Dandy was untied, while the men picked up their scythes and began mowing again. Clara and her father walked down the lane behind the cart. There was no need now to lead Dandy and urge her along. She knew she was going home, and they had to walk quite fast to keep up with her.

Back at the farm Clara's mother, Aunt Martha and Granny were waiting for them. On a low wall at the edge of the back yard they had placed a stone mortar or quern, which was like a basin. In it was another rounded stone with a handle. This was a kind of mill, for grinding the wheat that Clara and her father had brought from the harvest field.

Clara helped her mother and grandmother to snip the ears off the wheat-stalks in the sheaves and rub out the grains, allowing them to drop into a sieve on the table. Every now and again her mother took the sieve outside and blew the husks and chaff away, tossing the contents back into the sieve. When they had collected enough grains they poured them into the quern, and Aunt Martha began pounding and squeezing them with her pestle. It was hard work but she knew just how to go about it. She worked the heavy pestle round and round, giving the grain an occasional thump to make sure it was all being broken. Then she emptied the quern into a basin and called for more.

When it was all finished they emptied the basins into a clean flour bin. They now had a large amount of fine white flour instead of a heap of golden-brown wheat.

'Tomorrow we must make the bread,' said Clara's mother. The next day Clara watched as her mother, Granny and Aunt Martha started the bread-making. 'First we'll put the yeast on to work,' her mother explained.

She poured from the kettle half a pint of hand-hot water into a measure and added a teaspoonful of sugar. Then she poured it into a pint jug and crumbled about four ounces of yeast into it.

'Always allow room for the yeast to expand when it starts to work,' she told Clara.

It took about a quarter of an hour for the yeast to bubble and froth until it filled the jug. In the meantime the flour, now in a mixing bowl, had been put into the oven to warm up. Everything should be kept warm when making bread.

When the yeast was all dissolved and had formed a nice, thick foam, the flour was taken out of the oven. Clara's mother sprinkled it with salt and added a little butter, broken up fine. Then she made a hole in the middle of the flour and poured in the yeast.

Straight away she got busy with a wooden spoon, mixing the flour and yeast thoroughly and quickly. From time to time Granny took a warm cloth from the oven and wrapped it around the mixing bowl, to keep up the temperature. Presently the mixture was ready to be emptied on to a board sprinkled with flour. Clara's mother then stopped using the spoon and began to knead the mixture with her hands. It had by now turned into dough, and she was trying to get all the air out and to make sure it had the proper texture. When at last she was satisfied she put it in a warm bowl, covered it with a clean cloth and left it on a table near the fire to rise for about an hour until it had doubled in size.

Later she repeated the process. The dough was turned out on the kneading board again and vigorously kneaded for ten minutes. Clara's mother then cut it into convenient sizes for bread rolls and placed the lumps on a greased baking sheet. Once more a clean, damp cloth was placed over them, and they were left for a further three quarters of an hour, until again they had doubled their size.

Then into the hot oven they all went. Three quarters of an hour later they came out as brown loaves, beautifully crisp and warm and smelling as though they ought to be eaten straight away, with lashings of butter.

The following day was Sunday, a special Sunday—Lammas Day. The name, said Clara's mother, was really 'Loaf Mass', 'mass' being an old word for a festival, so it was the festival of the little loaves made from the first corn of the harvest.

All the loaves that had been baked the day before were placed in a big flat basket and taken to church. Everybody went to the service. The vicar, Rev Marcus Latimer, read a chapter from the Bible about how people were told to bring the first fruits of their harvest to God.

'"Thou shalt take of the first of all the fruit of the earth, which thou shalt bring of thy land which the Lord thy God giveth thee, and shalt put it in a basket and shalt go into the place which the Lord thy God shall choose to put his name there; and thou shalt go unto the priest that shall be in those days . . . And the priest shall take the basket out of thine hand and set it down before the altar of the Lord thy God . . ."'

When he had finished reading the people filed up to the front of the church, with their loaves in baskets. And the vicar took them and placed them before the altar, exactly as the Bible had said. Clara's father carried the family loaves in a big bread-basket, but Clara was also allowed to join the procession with a little basket of loaves, decorated with corn marigolds and poppies.

As they walked down the long churchyard path after the service Clara's brother, Giles, caught sight of a slow-worm slithering away among the gravestones. At once he went after it, grabbing here and there as it wriggled through the long grass. Clara stopped to watch him. All the family had walked on ahead, so there was no-one to tell them to come along and leave it alone.

Of course, Giles failed to catch it. The slow-worm was far too agile. But by the time he had finished searching for it the churchyard was empty, apart from two or three women gossiping by the lychgate.

Giles sat on a flat tombstone.

'If I had caught it,' he said, 'that would have been the first one this year. I could have taken it in and given it to old Latty. He could add it to his collection of first fruits.'

Clara giggled.

'I wonder what he does with all those loaves?' Giles said. 'If he eats all that lot they must last him for weeks.'

'I expect he takes them to the orphanage in town,' suggested Clara.

'Perhaps. Let's go and see what's happening to them now.'

Without waiting for an answer Giles started across the churchyard, dodging round some gravestones and leap-frogging over others. Clara followed. She was used to following Giles, who was two years older than she was, even though he often led her into trouble.

A path led from the vestry, at the back of the church, to the vicarage nearby. The vestry door was open, and so was the vicarage garden gate. Sounds of movement in the vestry suggested that the vicar was still there, tidying up. So Giles, making sure he was not being watched, slipped through the gate and into the garden. Clara joined him in a clump of laurel bushes.

'Look!' Giles pointed out.

On the lawn was a tea-table set for three—the vicar, his wife and his wife's sister who lived with them. On a plate by the silver teapot and best china tea-set were a plate of iced cakes, a dish of cream and a round basket holding some of the Lammas loaves.

'There you are! That's what happens to them,' said Giles.

Just then they heard sounds of something moving in the shrubbery. They peered anxiously, trying to see what it was. Then suddenly, Dandy appeared on the lawn.

'Goodness! She's escaped from the orchard!' exclaimed Clara. 'We must take her back.'

She was about to run on to the lawn, but Giles grabbed her arm.

'Wait,' he hissed . . . 'and shut up!'

Dandy trotted daintily across the lawn, making straight for the tea-table. Delicately she picked up one of the iced cakes and munched it. Then she turned her attention to the basket of little loaves and soon had her nose buried in it.

'We must stop her, Giles,' whispered Clara.

'Oh, must we? We shall no sooner be out on that lawn and someone will come out, and then we shall get the blame. They'll say we let her out, if nothing else.'

Clara had to admit that that was likely. Grown-ups were like that. Disasters were always somebody's fault, especially children's. And, anyhow, how could they explain what they were doing in the vicarage garden?

Footsteps came crunching along the path. Rev Marcus Latimer was returning from church. Giles and Clara crouched lower in the laurel thicket. A series of crashes came from the direction of the lawn. There were cries of dismay as Mrs Latimer and her sister came through the doorway from the drawing-room, while the vicar dashed on the lawn from the other direction. Peeping between the laurel leaves Clara and Giles saw Dandy standing amid the debris of the tea-table, placidly chewing the tablecloth.

'Let's get away while they're busy there,' urged Clara.

Giles agreed it might be a good idea.

'At least we know now who eats the Lammas loaves,' he laughed.

7 *September*

Harvest Home

'Harvest weather was never like this when I was a boy,' grumbled Clara's grandfather.

'I suppose the sun shone all the summer long, except for a shower or two on the grassfields when they needed rain,' her mother observed, sarcastically.

'Well, it didn't keep raining for weeks on end, like this year,' Grand-dad retorted. 'When was the last time we had a fine day?'

'Last Monday,' Clara's mother told him. 'I know that because I got my washing dried.'

Grand-dad refused to be comforted. 'That must have been the first time for a fortnight,' he groused. 'At this rate we shan't finish harvest till Christmas.'

However, as so often happens, a rainy August was followed by a serene September. Although the days grew shorter and heavy dews covered everything with water droplets until they evaporated in mid-morning, a big, glowing, orange Harvest Moon enabled the harvesters to work late at night. It rose above the horizon just about sunset and hung there like a great lantern, bathing the fields in a soft twilight. The air was fresh and crisp, and even the tired harvesters felt renewed vigour surging through them.

Field after field of wheat, oats and barley fell to the swishing scythe-blades of the reapers, as they advanced like the front line of an invading army. Behind them came a mixed company of helpers. The wives of the reapers, together with other housewives of the village and any old men who could still bend their backs in spite of rheumatism, gathered up the fallen stalks into bundles. Children of Clara's age (ten years) worked with them. Their task was to select six straight stalks and hand them to their mothers, who would twist them quickly around the bundles to fasten them into sheaves.

The sheaves had to be stood up on end, in groups of six or eight, leaning against each other, tent-like. They stayed there until they were thoroughly dry. Then the waggons, each drawn by a massive horse, were loaded with sheaves to be hauled down to the farmyard. Behind the buildings was a spacious rickyard where Clara's father, aided by a team of men, built rick after rick of sheaves. The ricks looked like rows of straw-coloured houses, each with straight sides and a neatly-sloped roof. Her father was an expert rick-maker. Later, when Eli could be spared from more urgent tasks, they would be thatched, for Eli was a skilled thatcher as well as being able to do many other jobs really well.

As for Clara, each fine afternoon she had to take the donkey cart with provisions to wherever the reapers were working. Dandy, who for the rest of the year did very little, grew tired of these daily journeys, and Clara had to keep prodding and shouting at her all the way to the field. She never had any trouble on the homeward journey, though. Dandy was always pleased to go home.

At last the men moved into the final field and the end of harvest was in sight. That afternoon when Clara and Dandy set out with the tea, Clara's father, leaving rick-making to Uncle Bart, came with them.

'I must be on hand for the cutting of the last sheaf,' he said. Her grandfather decided that he had to come, too.

Most of the other fields they passed had not only been mown but had been cleared of sheaves, and in some of them the gleaners were busy. These were mostly elderly women, widows and small children, who were picking up loose ears of corn that had fallen from the sheaves. The women had aprons of sacking with a pocket as wide as the apron in which they stored the grain they picked up or gleaned.

'They will glean enough grain for a good many loaves of bread,' Clara's father remarked. 'Nothing is wasted. The cottage bread-ovens will be busy this autumn.'

When they arrived at the last field the reapers had already mown most of it. They stopped for tea when Clara and her cart appeared.

'The last harvest picnic of the year,' said Uncle George, which made Clara feel rather sad. The harvest had seemed so long and difficult, but now that it was at an end she felt sorry. Very soon the fields would be bare and empty, the blackberries would be over, the swallows would have flown to Africa, and she would be back at school. She didn't look forward to that very much, even though she was heartily fed up with Dandy.

When the men had finished their meal Clara's father led the way to the final strip of standing corn.

'I suppose we must arrange this properly?' he said, looking at Eli.

'Aye, we must show proper respect,' Eli agreed. 'Best to pull our hats over our eyes.'

He did so, tilting the brim until he could see only the ground near his feet and the other men did the same. Then, bowing their heads and keeping their eyes fixed firmly on the ground, they started to mow. Never once did they look up.

With Toby sitting expectantly at her feet, Clara watched them advancing steadily towards the hedge, their scythes swinging rhythmically. Because their heads were bowed none of them noticed a fox poking his nose out at the end of the strip of corn. Toby did, though, and began to bark. Then, as the fox slunk out of the corn and ran away across the stubbles, Toby hurtled after it, yelping excitedly. Of course, the fox could run much faster than Toby, but the dog kept up the chase, still barking as they disappeared across the next field. Clara was the only person who saw the incident. The men all continued mowing.

The last corn-stalks fell. The men straightened their aching backs

and wiped the sweat from their faces. Eli and Clara's father carefully gathered up the stalks that had been severed by the last sweeps of the scythes and tied them into neat sheaves. As with the first sheaves of the harvest, these were stacked on Dandy's little cart and brought directly to the farm.

Later Clara found Eli sitting on a sack of corn in the barn, plaiting straw, which he was taking from those same sheaves. She watched and admired the way his deft fingers twisted and wove the straws without breaking them.

'What is it going to be?' she asked.

'This is the Kern Baby or Corn Dolly,' Eli told her. 'She's really the Corn Goddess. They used to say she was a very powerful spirit who put the life into the harvest.'

'And is she?'

'I don't rightly know. But 'tis as well to be on the safe side. Did you see how we pulled our hats down over our eyes when we cut the last strip of corn? Well, that was done for a reason. All through harvest we've cut the corn so that we finished each field near a gap in the hedge. That was so that if the Corn Spirit was in that field she could escape into the next. But when we came to the last strip she was bound to be in there. And there was nowhere else for her to go. So we covered up our faces as well as we could, so that she couldn't see whose scythe cut the corn-stalks which were her last refuge. She might not like it, see? She might take her revenge on that man.'

Clara nodded gravely.

'Now I've got those last stalks here. If there is a Corn Spirit this is where she must be. So we ought to make her look a bit like a goddess, eh?'

Clara thought that sounded reasonable.

'Perhaps she changed into a rabbit or a mouse and escaped that way,' she suggested. She nearly said 'a fox' but thought better of it.

'Maybe,' said Eli. 'I never thought of that.'

Eli's completed Corn Dolly had a long skirt, a cluster of wheat-ears for hair and a horn-shaped basket on one arm. She was a very dignified doll. Clara's grandmother placed her on the mantelpiece above the kitchen hearth.

'Is it true, all that Eli told me about the Corn Goddess?' Clara asked her.

'Who can say?' said her granny. 'That's what the old people used to say, and Eli believes it. Anyhow, he's made a nice dolly.'

Now that the reaping was finished, all the reapers turned their attention to helping the men who were carting sheaves to the rick-yard. That work went on twice as fast as before. Clara and Giles often spent the days riding on the waggons travelling between the fields and the ricks. On the empty waggons they sat on the sides, their legs dangling over the edge, but on the full ones they perched in a little nest right on the top of the load of sheaves. The men insisted that they stayed in the middle of the load, with their feet anchored by sheaves, lest they should fall off when the waggon bounced about over rough ground. When it was crossing ruts it swayed alarmingly, and on the approach to the rickyard it had to pass under the low boughs of a big elm-tree. Clara and Giles crouched with their heads in their arms, but even so the leaves tickled their faces.

Riding on top of the loads was fun. You could see for miles across the valley, where the other farms were also busy with the harvest. Everybody from the village seemed to be at work in the fields. Clara remembered her granny's saying when Mrs Vernditch, the baker's wife, had a baby girl last month.

'She's a real Betty Jarvis,' said Granny.

'What do you mean?' asked Clara.

Granny laughed.

'"Betty, Betty Jarvis,

Come about in harvest",' she recited. 'It means that she's a very thoughtless baby, to arrive when everybody's so busy.'

But they called the baby Louisa, not Betty.

One September afternoon the last sheaves were tossed on a waggon to be brought to the rickyard. This time Clara and Giles did not have the top of the load to themselves. All the men who had been working in the field climbed on, too. As the waggon trundled over the fields they stuck their hats on the prongs which they used for handling the sheaves and waved them high in the air.

'We've a-finished!' they shouted to the workers on the other farms. Their shouts echoed across the valley, and the other workers waved back.

At the rickyard the men working there joined in the rejoicing.

'Here it comes—the load we've been waiting for all the harvest!' they cried.

Old Peter pranced around, waving a sheaf on a prong.

'Let's have the Harvest Shout,' he called, and they all joined in.

'Well ploughed,

Well sowed,

Well harrowed,

Well mowed.

And all safely carted to the barn with never a load throwed!

Hip-hip-hip-hooray!'

'We ought to parade around the village with this last load, like they used to,' was Grand-dad's opinion. 'It's nice to show off a bit.'

'There'd be no-one to see us,' grinned Uncle George.

'Everybody's still at work in the fields. We're the first farm to finish.'

On the evening of the next day the Harvest Home Supper was held in the great barn. All day long preparations for it were going on. Clara's mother, grandmother and Aunt Martha made rabbit pies and meat pies, while at her home down the road Aunt Miriam roasted a huge joint of beef. Aunt Tillie, over at Parsonage Farm, had charge of the bread-making. Towards the end of the afternoon she arrived with several huge harvest loaves, crisp and brown and shaped like sheaves, with flowers among the wheat-ears. She had even moulded the figure of a little mouse running up the corn-stalks. Aunt Tillie also brought a batch of tarts and plum pies. Great bowls of potatoes had to be peeled and boiled, cabbages, beans and other vegetables cut and cooked, and two big cheeses brought up from the cellar.

Clara's task was fetching and carrying. She wanted to help with the cooking but was shooed away by the women, who were too busy to be bothered with her. Whenever she wandered off for a minute or two, however, the cry went up, 'Clara! Clara! Where's that girl now? Always disappears just when you want her.' Then Clara would come hurrying back, to be given the job of carrying crockery, knives and forks, mugs, apples and other accessories to the barn or of taking messages down the road to Aunt Miriam or Aunt Tillie or of emptying potato peelings and the outer leaves of cabbages into the boiler, for pig food.

In the barn men were erecting trestle tables and benches and festooning the beams and pillars with greenery and flowers. Strands of old man's beard and ivy were twined around the timbers and decorated with bunches of Michaelmas daisies and goldenrod and with sprays of berries. Little Tom, who liked arranging flowers, had filled two bowls with chrysanthemums and Michaelmas daisies to be placed in the middle of the table, near where Clara's father and grandfather would be sitting. Between the two vases was a wooden pedestal for the Corn Dolly.

Happily, the weather remained fine, so Clara was able to run all her errands without needing a raincoat and without getting her shoes muddy. She was still busy when the light faded and the great, glowing Harvest Moon appeared above the elm trees.

'No tea today,' declared her mother, when Clara complained that she was hungry. 'You must leave room for the Harvest Feast.'

So Clara found an apple to munch.

At last it was supper-time. Now Clara was dressed in her powder-blue coat trimmed with fur. Like everyone else, she had to wear her best clothes for this special occasion. Her father was dressed in knee-breeches, a tailed coat and a magnificent red waistcoat with silver brocade. Her mother, grandmother and aunts wore their Sunday dresses with big round brooches and bonnets with ribbons dangling. Even the farm workers had changed into their best corduroys and wore clean red handkerchiefs as cravats. Eli, who had made the Corn Dolly, had the privilege of carrying her to the barn and setting her on her pedestal. Baskets of fruit and loaves of bread were arranged around her, 'to remind her of what we expect of her next year,' Eli told Clara.

When everyone was seated, Clara's father said the grace and then everyone settled down to enjoy the feast. Oil-fired stable lanterns, swinging by chains from the rafters, threw an amber light over the merry scene. An hour or so later, when they had arrived at the bread and cheese course, her father announced the toasts, and everyone raised their mugs and drank to the Queen, the Harvest, the farmer, the farmer's wife and a dozen other worthies.

One of the toasts, recited by Mr Saunders, the blacksmith, was:

Let the wealthy and great
Live in splendour and state;
I envy them not, I declare it.
I eat my own lamb,
My own chicken and ham,
I shear my own fleece, and I wear it.
I have lawns; I have bowers;
I have fruit; I have flowers;
The lark is my morning alarmer.
So, jolly boys, now,
Here's God speed the plough.
Long life and good health to the farmer.

They all applauded and drank to the health of the farmer, Clara's father.

'It's time we opened another cider cask,' shouted Uncle George.

With so much ale and cider flowing, the men were raising their voices as they talked and were becoming flushed. Clara's mother signalled to her grandmother that it was time for little girls to go home.

'Oh no!' Clara objected. 'Let me stay just a little longer. Please.'

'Just a little longer, then,' agreed her granny, doubtfully.

Some of the trestle tables were now being swept clear and taken away to leave an open space for dancing. Old Peter had climbed to the threshing floor which formed a kind of raised platform at one end of the barn and, seated on a sack of wheat, was tuning his fiddle. From the gloom beyond the range of the flickering lanterns Little Tom staggered in with his big drum. Eli and James, who played in the village band, had brought their cornets, while Uncle Luther had a cello. From under his seat Grand-dad produced the strange, wiggly contraption of wood and leather which he called a 'serpent'. Clara had sometimes heard him trying to play it and producing a loud booming noise, like a distant bull bellowing.

'If anyone can play it they're welcome,' he used to announce. 'I can't. I haven't got enough wind.'

But now he intended to try again.

Giles and Uncle George were throwing rolls and crusts of bread at each other as the tables were being cleared. Toby and one or two other dogs who had been allowed in were retrieving them. They had been having as lavish a feast as anyone, from all the scraps that were thrown to them, but still seemed willing to find room for more. One roll of bread vanished into a gap between some sacks of corn piled against the threshing floor. Toby thrust his nose in, trying to reach it, then took a deep sniff and started barking.

'Poor old Toby! Can't you reach it?' said Clara.

Yanking him away by the collar, she knelt down and groped into the gap as far as her arm would reach.

'It's no good,' she said. 'I can't find it.'

As soon as she withdrew her hand Toby darted in again and started pawing vigorously at the sacks.

'Good dog, Toby,' cried Giles, arriving on the scene. 'What have you got? A rat? Let's get it out.'

'Oh, no, you don't!' exclaimed Uncle Bart, who was helping to arrange seats for everyone. 'We've got something better to do than ratting tonight. Hop it.'

And he pushed both Giles and Toby away. Clara, however, was still on her knees. She thought she had seen something moving behind those sacks and she wanted to take another look. With a hand shading her eyes from the light of the lanterns, she peered into the gloom beyond the sacks and under the raised threshing floor. Shafts of light piercing through cracks between the floor-boards illuminated segments of the narrow space. One of them fell on the unmistakable form of a crouching animal. At first Clara thought it was one of the cats. Then it moved and turned its head towards her, its eyes like lamps of glowing gold. It was a fox!

The fox? The one she had seen in the harvest field, escaping from the last strip of standing corn?

With thumping heart Clara knelt upright. She was about to shout out the news when she saw that the nearest person was Giles. He would want to start a fox hunt straight away, and Clara didn't want that.

'Out of the way, m'dear,' said Uncle Bart, shifting yet another sack. Clara moved, and the moment for revelation was past. She had made up her mind. The fox was her secret.

The musicians began to play some well-known songs first, for everyone to join in. They sang, with increasing volume, *The Farmer's Boy*, *Grandfather's Clock*, *Green Grow the Rushes-O* and other favourites. Then the band switched to dance music. Clara's father ceremoniously invited her mother to join him in the first dance, and soon the aunts and uncles and the workmen and their wives were joining them on the floor. The noise shook cobwebs from the rafters and set the lanterns jigging as vigorously as the dancers. Clara had a few dances, with Uncle George and Emmie and some of the other children. Then, as the revelry became more boisterous, Clara's grandmother signalled that it was time for the children to go home,

and Clara knew that this time she meant it.

'We've left the Corn Dolly in the barn,' she remembered as she and Granny crossed the yard. 'Won't she get damaged?'

'No. No matter how wild they get, they'll take care she doesn't get hurt,' Granny assured her. 'She'll be back safe on the mantelpiece tomorrow morning.'

'What happens to her in the end?'

'Oh, when the ploughs start work again after the Christmas break we have a special day called Plough Monday,' Granny explained. 'That's the first Monday after Twelfth Night. And when they've turned the first furrow they place the Corn Dolly in it and bury her. You see, the men believe—or at least some of them do—that the Corn Spirit lives in the cornfields and gives life to the seed and so produces a harvest. She was in the last stalks of standing corn, and that is why they were woven into the form of a dolly. In the New Year she goes back into the soil to start her work all over again.'

Clara pondered. It all seemed sensible enough. If there was a Corn Spirit that would be the way to catch and tame her. But, as she dropped off to sleep presently, with the sounds of revelry from the barn still resounding from the far side of the yard and with the moonbeams bathing her bed in a cold light, she couldn't help wondering a little about that fox.

8 *September*

Michaelmas

Clara was crying. 'It's not fair,' she sobbed.

'But surely you knew that Toby really belonged to old Peter?' said her mother.

'No, I didn't! Nobody ever told *me*.'

'I dare say the child's right,' her granny interposed. 'Toby's been living in the house ever since she can remember.'

'Of *course* he has. And now he's got to go.' And Clara broke into another flood of tears.

It was indeed a sad occasion. Old Peter, who had been spending his time doing odd jobs of various kinds around the house and farmyard, such as drawing water from the well, chopping firewood, turning the butter-churn and feeding the calves, felt that he was at last too old for work. He was retiring. His daughter, who lived in another village forty miles away, had offered him a home. He was going to live with her, and he was taking Toby.

Seven or eight years earlier someone had given Toby to Peter as a puppy. The dog used to come with Peter to the farmyard every morning and almost at once he showed interest in the sheep. He used to leave Peter to his pottering about the farmyard and instead followed Clara's father when he went around the farm.

'He's a born sheep-dog,' said Clara's father.

So Toby took to living at the farm, where he was fed every morning and evening and where he slept by the hearth in the big living room. He adopted Clara's father as his master, and everyone was content.

But now that old Peter was going away he wanted to take Toby with him.

'I've got to get rid of my few sticks of furniture,' he said. 'If I don't take the old dog I shan't have anything to remind me of home.'

'He's got every right to, of course,' Clara's father agreed, though he was very sorry to lose Toby. 'We shall have to get another dog. Perhaps we can buy one at Norchester Goose Fair.'

'It won't be the same,' lamented Clara. 'Can't we buy Toby from old Peter?'

But she knew that old Peter would never sell him.

'We must take your ram to the fair,' said her father, changing the subject and trying to cheer her up. 'He's about ready to go.'

The lamb which Clara and Giles had rescued from the snow in February and which Clara had reared on the bottle was now a fine, upstanding ram.

'He's worth two guineas of anyone's money,' said Grand-dad.

'Pet lamb, spoilt ram,' quoted Granny. 'He's been spoilt right enough. Someone's going to have trouble with him.'

'So long as they don't bend down with their back towards him they'll be all right,' Grand-dad chuckled.

Clara listened mournfully. She didn't mind parting with Sooty the ram, because he was getting too strong for her to handle, and anyway she had always known that he would have to be sold. But she wouldn't have parted with Toby for any number of guineas.

Clara's father had a big batch of sheep to take to Norchester Goose Fair. Although it was called a Goose Fair, because in times past it had been noted for fat geese, Norchester Fair was now a fair for the exchange of all kinds of farm animals, especially sheep. Here farmers bought and sold the ewes and rams which would be the parents of next year's lambs. So Clara's father and Uncle Jonah had picked out seventy of their best ewes for sale at the fair.

Clara and Giles were sent to bed early the night before the fair. While there were still several hours of darkness to come, Clara was awakened by the bleating of sheep, milling around in the yard. Downstairs she found that Giles had already been up for half-an-hour and was finishing a big breakfast of eggs, bacon and fried bread.

'You'll need your coats and scarves,' said their mother. 'I think there's a frost this morning.'

Giles was to help Uncle Jonah and Uncle George drive the sheep to the fair. The yellow light from the lamps threw a golden glow over the flock and its attendants as Clara stood at the door watching them move off. A few of the sheep tried to dodge back and escape into the orchard but the dogs soon rounded them up and drove them back to the others.

'It's a good thing they still have Toby,' Clara's mother remarked. Clara nodded, not trusting herself to speak. The other dogs were good with sheep, but none was quite like Toby.

The bleating faded as the sheep trotted away along the lane. Clara looked up at the sky. Only a few of the crystal-bright stars were hidden by a single small cloud, but thin wisps of ground mist came drifting across the yard.

'Signs of a fine day,' said her father. 'Come and have breakfast, Clara. We must be away in good time, too.'

He was travelling to the fair this year not on horseback, as he usually did, but by pony and cart, because he was taking Sooty, Clara's pet ram. Sooty had not been brought up with the flock and so couldn't be trusted with them now. Besides, as a special ram he had to arrive looking at his best, not sprinkled with leaves, grass stalks and seeds. Sooty had been given his name when, as a small lamb, he had a black face, black ears and black feet 'just as though he had been dipped in a soot bag' as Uncle Jonah had put it. Now those parts of him were still black, but his fleece was a lovely creamy white, and so his name didn't suit him as well. He really was a magnificent animal.

Sooty was lifted into the pony-cart and tethered by a rope halter to the back of the driver's seat. A rope net was spread over him and fastened to the sides, to prevent him from trying to jump out. Clara's father sat in the driver's seat, holding the pony's reins, and Clara sat next to him, huddling close to him with a warm rug tucked around her legs. The seat on the other side was occupied by old Peter, in his best overcoat and holding a rush dinner-basket under his arm. Sooty shared the back of the cart with a sack of corn which was to be delivered to Clara's aunt Gertrude in Norchester, a crate containing twelve cockerels (for sale at the fair) and two wooden chests in which all old Peter's possessions had been packed. Clara sat there glumly, closer to her father than to Peter. She loved old Peter in a way. He had been a part of the farm ever since she could remember, and he had always been kind to her, even though sometimes he was a bit grumpy. Perhaps because she was fond of him she was angry with him for going away. She certainly could not forgive him for taking Toby.

As the pony, Gipsy, trotted along the gravel lanes a pale streak in the east gradually spread over the whole sky, and the countryside became visible again. There were no horizons. The pearly-grey sky merged with the pearly-grey mist that covered the fields like a lake. If we were standing on the hill, thought Clara, we would see the tops of the trees jutting above the mist like islands, but down here we are at the bottom of the lake. Everything was swathed in gossamer, too. Millions of tiny spiders must have been at work, spinning the strands of silky web which clung to every bush, bramble and grass-stem. A man they saw herding up cows in a field, no doubt to take them to a shed for milking, was wading knee-deep through gossamer.

'There ought to be mushrooms about,' observed Clara's father. 'We must go and look in the meadows tomorrow morning.'

The fair was held in the great market-place of Norchester. About half the area was occupied by hurdle-pens containing thousands of sheep. New flocks were still arriving, and the air was filled with their bleating and with the shouts of shepherds and the barking of dogs. Another section of the market-place was devoted to cattle, and yet another to scores of pens of poultry, mostly cockerels and turkeys. There were lots of geese as well but most of these were not penned but were tethered to railings by lengths of string fastened to their

RISING
SUN
the
FOX

legs. Clara was amused to see that some of them were wearing little boots of soft leather.

'They have come a long way,' her father explained, 'perhaps a hundred miles or more, and they've been travelling for weeks. They travel slowly, of course, feeding on grains dropped in the harvest fields, but some of them develop sore feet.'

Along one side of the market was an iron rail, supported by iron posts, and here a score or two of great cart-horses and many more ponies were tethered. As Clara arrived, so from another direction did a drove of wild ponies, chased along one of the narrow streets by men who looked like gipsies. They were young ponies which had been bred on the moors and had run wild there all the summer. Now the time had come for them to be trained for their life's work.

Besides all the animals there were many stalls of canvas and timber, where men or women were selling sweets, cakes, ribbons, buttons, bonnets, knives and many other things. A foreign-looking man, no taller than Clara, was playing a hurdy-gurdy, while a monkey in a red hat, perched on his shoulder, held out a tin to collect pennies. There were coconut-shies, boxing booths, fortune-tellers and a bewildering selection of other things to see and do.

Clara's father drove Gipsy along a road at the edge of the market and down a side-street to an inn called the Wheelwright's Arms. Here he was greeted by the owner, whom he evidently knew very well, for he addressed him by his Christian name, Arthur. The pony was unharnessed and put into a stable, with a nosebag of oats to keep her happy. The cart was parked in the inn yard.

'I put up here whenever I come to Norchester,' her father told Clara.

He, Clara and old Peter left the cart and its contents in the charge of Arthur, while they made their way to the market-place to find Uncle Jonah, George and Giles. It seemed a hopeless task, in all those confused and noisy crowds, but her father had a good idea where to look. Soon they were looking over the hurdles into the pens which held their sheep. There were seven pens, with ten sheep in each, and a little one at one end for Sooty. Clara thought all the sheep looked very attractive and well-fed, and her father seemed very well pleased.

'Well now,' he said, serving out orders. 'I'll be staying here and bargaining with buyers. George and Giles, go back to the cart and fetch Sooty here. Jonah, you go with Peter to find Mr Nathaniel Merryweather's cart at the London Road Inn. If it's there, take Peter's boxes and stow them in it. If not, leave them with the landlord. That's Mr Robert Golding. Mention my name and tell him to take good care of them. Clara, you stay here with me, and don't go out of my sight.'

Clara wondered whether she now had to say goodbye to Peter, but her father said,

'No, we shall all have a bite of dinner together at the Wheelwright's Arms.'

'Will Peter go all the way in Mr Merryweather's cart?'

'No, only as far as Chettletown. His daughter lives in a village five miles beyond that. But he'll find another carrier's van at Chettletown. It's all been arranged.'

Clara thought what a good thing it was that her father knew so many people and could arrange things so well. She knew she would never be half as efficient.

When they all met again at the Wheelwright's Arms for a dinner of bread and cheese and lardy cake most of the business of the day had already been completed. The sheep had been sold for a good price. A farmer had paid three guineas, not two, for Sooty. A poulterer had purchased the cockerels and had taken them away. Old Peter had been introduced to Mr Merryweather and the boxes had been transferred to his cart. After they had finished eating, all the men shook hands with Peter and wished him well. Peter replied gruffly. He didn't want to talk much. When it was Clara's turn he stooped down and kissed her. Clara turned her cheek to be kissed but she didn't put her arms around his neck or kiss him back. She was feeling too sad. Nor did she go to the stables to say goodbye to Toby, who was tied up there with the other dogs. She was afraid that if she did she would cry again.

Her father sensed how she was feeling so he took her back to the fair.

'Now, how shall we spend some of that money you got for

Sooty?' he enquired.

So they bought some 'fairings', which are flat gingerbread cakes sold at fairs, and some new gloves for Clara, and some ribbons and a glass paperweight with flowers inside it for her mother, and a pincushion with thimbles and pins for her granny, and then her father made her stop buying presents.

'You can't buy presents for everyone,' he laughed, 'or you won't have any money left.'

Clara would have liked to buy for Giles one of the knives with which a stallholder, standing on a box and shouting at the top of his voice, sliced leather, paper and planks a half-inch thick.

'If Giles wants one, let him buy it for himself,' said her father. 'He has some money of his own.'

Later they found that Giles had bought one of the knives, but it was so blunt that it wouldn't cut anything till they had sharpened it with a grindstone for half an hour.

Clara wanted to know about the lines of men and girls standing on the steps of a big building known as the Corn Exchange.

'They are workers looking for a new job,' her father told her. 'You see that some of the men are wearing a whip-cord in their hats—those are carters who work with horses. Then there are the shepherds, who wear wool in their hats and carry their crooks, and those girls holding mops want domestic work. Norchester Fair is what is called a Hiring Fair, or sometimes a Mop Fair.'

'Do other places have fairs like this?'

'Oh yes, it's a general custom at Michaelmas fairs. Michaelmas is the time when farm rents are paid and when people change jobs. It's not only sheep and other animals that move from place to place at Michaelmas; it's people, too.'

'Are you going to hire someone else to do Peter's work?'

'Not here. I'm going to arrange for John Downer, from the village, to come over to the farm every day to take over Peter's jobs. John is lame but he can manage that.'

Then, suddenly, Clara saw something and immediately fell in love with it. It was a tiny, gentle, creamy-brown cow, tied to a tethering ring in a side wall of the Corn Exchange.

'Oh, what a beauty! Whatever sort of cow is that?'

All the cattle on the farm were brown and white or red and white, and much larger than this dainty little thing.

'It's a Jersey,' her father told her. 'She comes from the island of Jersey, over towards France. There aren't many of her sort about in these parts.'

'I *would* like her,' sighed Clara, wistfully.

A man appeared from the crowd.

'Want to buy her, Guvnor?' he asked. 'She's a beauty.'

Clara looked at her father and saw that he was interested.

'Shall we?' he asked her.

'Oh yes!' said Clara, ecstatically.

'She's in calf,' the man informed them. 'She'll calve in about three months' time.'

'She would do very well for a house cow, to supply us with milk for the house,' her father thought aloud. 'Jerseys give very rich milk; lots of cream in it.'

So he and the man got down to bargaining, and before long Clara's father had bought the cow. When the business was concluded they untied the rope which fastened her to the wall, and Clara was allowed to lead her back to the Wheelwright's Arms. Clara thought she had never seen a lovelier little cow. She had a black muzzle, and dainty limbs, and big brown eyes, like a deer's, with long black eyelashes. She walked very quietly and docilely by Clara's side, as though realizing she was in good hands.

'I'm going to call you Fairy,' Clara told her.

When they arrived at the Wheelwright's Arms the man Arthur greeted her father.

'I've got what you wanted,' he told him.

From behind the bar he dragged out a grey and white puppy, plump and roly-poly but shivering with fear.

'Will he do?' he asked.

'I should think so,' said her father. 'What about it, Clara? We need another dog in place of Toby.'

Clara knew that no other dog would ever replace Toby, but she felt very sorry for this sad little puppy.

'Poor little thing! He's frightened,' she exclaimed, stooping to comfort him.

The puppy licked her hand, snuggled up against her dress and looked up into her face. So that decided that.

All that remained now was to arrange for taking the new cow, Fairy, home. She had to walk, of course, and Uncle George was given the job of leading her. Clara would have liked to, but her father said it was too far.

'But I walked all the way here,' objected George.

'Your legs are younger than mine and Jonah's,' her father told him. 'You'll be home before dark.'

He didn't have even Giles for company, for her father could see that Giles was tired, too. So Clara, Giles and Uncle Jonah rode home with her father in the pony-cart, Clara nursing the new puppy all the way.

'Whatever will the man bring home next!' exclaimed her mother, when she saw the puppy and heard about the cow. But she soon produced a bowl of warm milk for the puppy, after which the puppy itself decided that Toby's blanket behind father's armchair would make an ideal bed. It soon curled up there and went to sleep.

That is not quite the end of Clara's Michaelmas story.

Two days later, not long after Clara's mother had shut the back door for the night, they heard a vigorous scratching outside.

'Now what in the world is that?' said Granny.

'Better go and see,' said Clara's father.

With a sigh, Clara's mother got up from her chair, where she had just settled for the evening, and went over to the door.

The moment she opened it in bounded . . . Toby!

Wagging his tail and wriggling his whole body he dashed across to Clara's father, licked his hand and tried to climb on his lap.

'Goodness gracious!' exclaimed Granny. 'How ever did you get here?'

'I reckon he walked,' said Grand-dad.

Clara was overjoyed to see him again.

Toby was very tired, but he managed to eat a big plateful of food before he tottered over to his old blanket and fell into a blissful sleep. The fact that the blanket was occupied by the new puppy made no difference. Toby simply flopped down on top of him. The puppy, with a squeak, wriggled out from underneath and then dropped off to sleep again, close against Toby's back.

Four days after that they had another surprise. Old Peter walked into the kitchen!

'What in the world . . . !' began Clara's mother.

''Tis no good, Missus,' old Peter said apologetically, 'I couldn't stay there. It wasn't home. This is where I belong, and this is where I'm going to stay till I die.'

'How did you get here?' Clara asked. 'You didn't *walk*, like Toby?'

'No, I came the same way as I went. I got lifts in carts.'

'What about your boxes?'

'Oh, they'll be coming later. And I don't mind if they don't, as long as I'm here.'

Clara's father smiled when he heard what had happened.

'Well, his old cottage down the road is still empty; he can have that,' he said, 'but he hasn't any furniture left. He got rid of it all.'

'I'll put him in the spare room for a few days till we get things sorted out,' said Clara's mother.

'I don't reckon I'm too old to do a bit of work, after all,' Peter decided. 'I dare say I can manage to weed the garden and draw buckets of water and chop wood and turn that old butter churn.'

'We've got a new cow for you to milk, as soon as she has her calf,' said Granny.

'And I can do that,' declared old Peter. 'And rear the calf, too.'

So that was how old Peter and Toby came home. And why there were two dogs now sleeping on the blanket behind Clara's father's armchair.

9 *October/November*

Hallowe'en

All day long a gale from the south-west had hurled rain against the windows as though it intended to smash them. At times a swirling gust came sweeping down the chimney, driving an eddy of choking smoke into the room. Then raindrops would sputter down and hiss as they turned to steam in the log fire.

Fortunately it was possible to get to the woodshed from the kitchen without going outdoors. Clara slipped through the connecting door from time to time during the afternoon to see how her grandfather was getting on. Sitting with his legs on either side of a long wooden stool, as near to the outer door as possible, for he needed all the light he could get, he was carving a 'punkie lantern' from a big mangold. He should have been using a pumpkin or a turnip, but the pumpkins had failed this year and the turnips were not large enough. The mangold, however, was just right as well as being a lovely orange-golden colour.

Grand-dad first up-ended the mangold and cut four inches off the bottom. Setting aside that piece for a lid, he then scooped out the inside of the root until it was quite hollow. The shell he left around it was about an inch thick.

On one side he cut out two eyes, a triangular hole for a nose, and a long curved slit for a mouth. In the bottom he gouged out a hole for a candle to stand in. Pieces of matches, the long kind called lucifers, served as teeth. More pieces of match-sticks were used to fasten the lid to the head, and Clara's punkie lantern was complete; all he had to do now was to light the candle.

'Oh, it's a really lovely one!' exclaimed Clara. 'Thank you, Grand-dad,' and she gave him an enthusiastic kiss. Grand-dad grinned with pleasure.

'I doubt whether you'll be able to take it out tonight, though, my lady,' he told her.

'Never mind,' said Clara, 'Uncle George says if it keeps on raining we'll have the bonfire tomorrow night.'

At tea-time her father and Uncle George came in, dripping wet and muddy. Aunt Martha looked with disapproval at the mud their boots left on the kitchen floor and opened her mouth to reprimand them. Then she thought better of it and turning her back on them, carried on with peeling potatoes at the kitchen sink.

'Talk about vexing!' Clara's father exclaimed to her mother, who had just entered the room. 'We brought all the young cattle from the downs down the drove to the yard and then they all dodged back again.'

'It was old Peter's fault,' said George. 'He didn't get the gate shut quickly enough. One dodged back and they all followed.'

'You ought to have shut the gate yourself,' his father told him. 'You know you can't rely on old Peter to move any faster than an ox-cart. . . .'

'Where are they now?' put in Clara's mother, in order to change the subject and avoid an argument.

'Up on the hill again. And there they can stay till tomorrow. If they choose to stay out in this weather rather than bed down in a barn all freshly littered up with clean straw, that's their hard luck.'

'Go and get changed, the pair of you,' said Clara's mother. 'Your clothes are starting to steam in this warm kitchen.'

After tea, people started to arrive. Those whom Clara was most pleased to see were her best friends, Sarah and Emmie. Stephen Harrasmith and Dickie Vell, Giles' friends, came, too, and there were several aunts and uncles as well.

'It looks as though we're going to have to spend our Hallowe'en indoors,' said Clara's mother.

'I think it may clear up soon,' replied Uncle Bart, who was just taking off his wet raincoat. 'There are some breaks in the clouds.'

'Well, have a drink,' Clara's father invited them, and he ladled out hot punch from the big mixing-bowl into pewter mugs.

'And we'll have some Hallowe'en games,' declared little Aunt Miriam, who was lively and energetic. 'Let's try apple-bobbing. Where's that big bucket, Martha?'

The table was pushed back and the big bucket, filled nearly to the brim with water, was placed in the middle of the room.

'Who wants to be first?' asked Aunt Miriam, and when all the boys shouted 'Me!' they decided it should be Giles. While he was being blindfolded and his hands tied behind his back, Uncle George selected some of the best eating apples.

'Which girl does he like?' he enquired. 'Ah, this one we'll mark for Sarah. And this one for Emmie.'

'He likes Julie Tiverton, down at the mill,' said Clara.

'I don't!' protested Giles.

'Good. This one for Julie,' said George, making a mark on it with his knife. 'And we'll have one for Stephen's big sister, Ellen.'

'Put one in for me,' urged Clara.

'Oh, all right,' said George. 'But there shouldn't really be one for his sister.'

When all the apples had been placed in the bucket and were floating on the surface of the water Giles was made to kneel in front of it. Then, blindfolded and with his hands tied behind his back, he had to try to grab one of the apples with his teeth. Watching him splashing about and getting the water up his nose was good fun, and it took him a long time to capture an apple.

'Whose is it?' everybody asked.

George examined the markings.

'It looks like Clara's,' he said.

'That's not fair. He's not supposed to choose his sister,' objected Aunt Miriam.

'Well, I don't like *her*, that's sure,' declared Giles. 'But I don't like any of the others, either!' he added.

Clara, when it was her turn, got her teeth into an apple marked for Stephen Harrasmith.

'Ha-ha! I knew it!' crowed Giles, and Clara blushed, because she thought she didn't like Stephen Harrasmith at all . . . well, only a little bit. But it was a lovely apple.

After all the young ones had had their turn, they tried apple-peeling. Each one in turn tried to peel an apple so that the peel was in one unbroken piece. Then the peel had to be thrown over the left shoulder and when it landed on the floor it would form the initial of one's true love.

'Mine is a G!' said Clara, examining her peel. 'That must be Uncle George.'

'It's not,' said Giles. 'It's an S. It's Stephen again!'

And Stephen gave him a good punch.

'It's silly, anyway, playing all these games for sweethearts,' said Giles. 'It's as bad as playing kissing games at Christmas.'

'Hallowe'en is the time for this sort of game,' Aunt Miriam explained. 'It's the time when you can most easily look into the future and see what's going to happen. There are all sorts of ways of doing it. If on Hallowe'en you go into the garden at midnight and pick nine sage leaves, one on each of the first nine strokes of the church clock, a vision of your future husband will appear.'

'Did you do that, Aunt Miriam?' Clara asked.

'I did,' said her aunt.

But Uncle Bart, her husband, said, 'You knew very well I was just coming through the door into the garden.'

Aunt Miriam laughed. 'Let's try roasting some nuts on the hearth,' she said, changing the subject.

Just then Uncle Luther looked in.

'Are you going to stay indoors all the evening?' he enquired. 'No bonfire?'

'Why? Has it stopped raining?' they cried.

'Half an hour ago,' he assured them. 'It's a lovely clear night.'

Immediately everyone started bustling about, putting on coats and boots and looking for scarves and gloves.

'Better let me light the candle for you,' said Grand-dad, as he fetched Clara's punkie lantern from the woodshed. When he had lit it and had pegged the lid on with several pieces of match-sticks the golden light shone most satisfactorily through the holes he had cut for eyes, nose and mouth. He had also fixed a wire handle so that Clara could carry it easily.

'Haven't you got a punkie lantern?' Clara asked Giles, but he only looked glum and didn't answer.

Ever since harvest old Peter and Little Tom had been spending most of their time cutting hedges and tidying up the farm. All the bushes and dead wood they had cut had been carted to Nut Hill, on the side of the farm nearest the village. Because the hill was so steep it grew only grass and was never ploughed. On its flat summit was a grassy tumulus or barrow, where someone, ages ago, had been buried, and the bonfire was always built around it.

'In the old days,' said Clara's grandfather, 'they used to make the cows walk through the ashes when the fire died down but they don't do it now. They used to say it protected animals against disease.' Clara had heard this story before, but she said nothing.

The way to Nut Hill was a muddy sunken lane, with yew trees growing on high banks on either side. It was an eerie place. The yew tree branches met overhead to blot out the sky, so that under them it was gloomy even on a sunny afternoon. The dark trees on the left-hand bank were growing in the churchyard.

Most of the men had gone on ahead, so when Clara, Emmie and Sarah came near the churchyard they began to feel nervous.

'Let's wait for Grand-dad,' Clara suggested, so they stopped for a moment. The wind was still strong enough to shake the tree branches overhead till they seemed to be whispering to each other. A sudden sharp howl or yell made them move a little closer together.

'It's a fox,' said Emmie, but Sarah thought it was an owl in the churchyard.

Suddenly a far more blood-curdling shriek came from the churchyard yews. Then another from the trees on the opposite side of the lane. Then another, just ahead.

'Look!' cried Clara. There, moving through the dark foliage, were glowing eyes. For a few moments they were there; then they vanished and more appeared among the trees opposite. The wild scream was repeated.

The three girls grabbed each other and stood there, trembling. They wanted to run but were not sure which way to go.

'Let's go back home,' whispered Sarah, as the lights continued to flit about and the ghostly yells continued. Then they heard slow steady footsteps approaching. The ghost, or whatever it was, yelled again just as the footsteps were near enough for the girls to decide that they belonged to Clara's grandfather.

'Oh Grand-dad! What is it?' cried Clara, seizing his hand.

Grand-dad stopped and surveyed the wayward lights.

'Now then, you boys! That's enough of that! Stop it!' he shouted.

'Ohhh, was it them?' exclaimed Clara.

For answer came a mocking chant, as the boys fled up the lane.

'Moonlight, starlight,

Bogeys won't be out tonight,' they carolled.

'You thought they were, though, didn't you?' came Giles's voice.

'I'll skin him!' said Clara. 'And I thought he didn't have a punkie lantern.'

'How did they make them keep appearing and disappearing?' Sarah wondered.

'By hiding them under their coats,' Grand-dad told her. 'Now hurry, or they'll be lighting the bonfire.'

Clara's father was about to do so when they came to the end of the lane, opened a field gate and climbed to the top of the little hill. Scores of people were gathered around the pyre. Although the bushes were wet, heaps of dry straw had been fetched and piled around them. The straw burned fiercely as soon as a light was applied and before long the bonfire was well alight. As the flames shot up they revealed the effigy of a guy, with a rocket in each hand and a Catherine Wheel on the front of his hat, fixed firmly

to a stake in the middle.

'November 5th is really Guy Fawkes' Night,' said Clara's grandfather, 'but we've always had our bonfire on Hallowe'en and we can't have two. There wouldn't be enough bushes.'

When the fire was burning most fiercely some of the young men dipped besoms into a tar-barrel and held them in the flames until they caught fire. Then they ran about, waving the burning brooms and shouting. It was rather alarming, and Clara kept close to her grandfather.

'They're supposed to be frightening witches away,' he explained. 'I doubt whether they really believe in witches, but they enjoy it.'

Once the guy had collapsed into the centre of the fire and had been completely consumed, people began to let off more fireworks. There were rockets, Roman candles, jumping jacks, magnesium flares, bangers and all kinds of other fireworks. Some of them propelled balls of coloured light high into the air, to explode and send down showers of smaller globes. Clara enjoyed those, but the boys liked the noisy ones better. They threw their punkie lanterns into the bonfire so that they would have more freedom in chasing each other. Clara couldn't make up her mind to do that, though, after her grandfather had taken so much trouble in making it.

'I'm not going back along that lane,' declared Clara when the bonfire burned low and it was time to go home.

'We'll go *through* the churchyard, then,' said her grandfather, 'and out on to the hard road. It's a bit farther but not nearly so muddy.'

The paths were paved, but it was still creepy in the churchyard. The owl was still hooting and some of the newer gravestones were ghostly white in the starlight. When the wind stirred the distant bonfire and prompted flames to spurt up they were reflected on the stones, which appeared to waver and move. The marble figure of an angel stooping over one grave seemed alive.

Suddenly another figure nearby really did move. Grand-dad seized Clara and Sarah by the arm and drew them into the shadow of a yew tree, with Emmie.

'Sssh,' he cautioned.

Keeping completely still, they watched the mysterious figure. It was a woman. She had tucked into the angle of one arm a bowl or basin. With the other hand she made peculiar motions, as though she were sowing seed, as she walked quietly along the path. The girls could see that her lips were moving.

'It's . . . it's Aunt Martha,' gasped Clara, stifling an impulse to shout. Her grandfather put his hand over her mouth.

When Aunt Martha had disappeared around the corner of the church, Grand-dad made them all hold hands and, taking the lead, guided them across the dark churchyard to a stile which led to the road. When they arrived there, he started chuckling.

'What was that about?' asked Clara. 'What was she doing?'

'Fancy our Martha doing that!' chuckled Grand-dad. 'Fancy our Martha!'

'Doing what?' demanded Clara.

'She was sowing hemp seed,' Grand-dad explained. 'Or rather, she was rehearsing. She'll do the actual sowing at midnight. If you could have heard what she was reciting it would have been this:

Hemp seed I sow,
Hemp seed I hoe,
In hopes my true love will come after me and mow.'

'So it's like apple-bobbing?' said Emmie.

'It serves the same purpose. When she does it at midnight if she looks over her left shoulder after she has repeated the rhyme three times she hopes to see the ghost of her future husband following her with a scythe! But fancy our Martha doing that! Well, well!'

'She's too old to get married,' said Clara. 'She must be at least forty.'

'You'd better not let her hear you say that,' said Grand-dad. 'She evidently doesn't think so. Perhaps I ought to go and put Henry Gray wise to what's happening. He's taken rather a fancy to her.'

As they trudged back along the road to the farm the night was punctuated with the explosions of more fireworks while other bonfires threw a dusky glow into the dark sky. Nearly all were dying down, but one straight ahead seemed to be flaring up. Suddenly flames shot high into the air and Grand-dad exclaimed:

'Great heavens! A building's on fire!'

'It's one of ours!' cried Clara.

They were soon able to see that it was the barn, with its yard and cattle-pens, on the far side of the farmstead. Men were rushing hither and thither with buckets of water, but the fire evidently had a good hold. As they hurried to the scene the thatched roof went up in a sheet of flame far bigger than their Hallowe'en bonfire.

Fortunately the wind was blowing the flames away from the house and other buildings, so there was little danger of their catching fire. Clara's father and all the men carried buckets of water up ladders, though, and poured it over the thatch, as a precaution. No-one went to bed until well after midnight, and some of the men stayed up all night, keeping watch.

'How did it happen?' asked Clara.

'We don't know,' said her grandmother. 'Perhaps a rocket landed in the thatch. Perhaps some of the boys were playing about there with fireworks. Dangerous things, I always say.'

'What a good thing your father couldn't get those cattle to go into the barn!' said Grand-dad. 'They might have got burnt.'

'Do you think they knew?'

'It's possible. Animals do have strange premonitions. And not only on Hallowe'en.'

10 *December*

Christmas

Two weeks before Christmas the family had reason to be glad that Toby had come back. In the middle of the night Clara was awakened by his frantic barking; the puppy tried to join in, though he couldn't make half as much noise as Toby. Clara heard bedroom doors opening and shutting and heavy feet shuffling along the passage.

'Drat that dog!' said her father's voice. 'What's the matter with you, Toby?'

Clara crept out of bed, slipped into her red flannel dressing-gown and went across to the window. A waning moon illuminated the farmyard with a ghostly twilight. The world looked tranquil and quiet, but when she opened the window a cacophony of sound poured in. Geese were honking, turkeys gobbling, hens cackling, cows lowing, and, as she listened, Dandy the donkey joined in with a prolonged bray.

Other members of the family became aware of the disturbance at the same moment, and within minutes the house was filled with voices and the sound of scurrying feet. Lights shone from the downstairs windows and very soon the back door opened and Clara saw her father, grandfather and Uncle George emerge, each carrying a gun. Toby was bounding along, barking and running in circles because he wasn't sure where they were going, and the puppy, whom Clara had named Pudge, was excitedly joining in. Clara's granny, in nightdress, dressing-gown and slippers, came into Clara's bedroom.

'What a rumpus!' she exclaimed.

'What is it? A fox getting at the turkeys?' Clara asked.

'Must be,' said her granny. 'I don't know what good taking their guns will do them. They can't see well enough to shoot in this light.'

'Perhaps they'll just fire a gun into the air, to frighten the fox away,' Clara suggested.

'There's enough noise going on out there already to frighten a fox into the next county,' declared her granny.

'Look!' exclaimed Clara, suddenly. 'There's a man!'

She pointed to a furtive figure slinking around a corner of one of the sheds.

'Where? I can't see anyone.'

'He's gone now. I just caught a glimpse of him disappearing around that corner.'

'No, I never saw him. My eyes aren't as good as they used to be,' admitted Granny.

When the men returned, without having fired a shot, Clara told them about the man she had seen.

'So it wasn't a fox, after all,' said her father.

'I'll bet it was a gipsy. There are some camping up in Whiteshoot Hollow, in the chalk-pit,' said Uncle George.

'I'll be glad when the poultry are off our hands,' said her father. 'They're always a worry, just before Christmas, when they're fat and ready for market.'

Preparing the Christmas poultry occupied much of the week before Christmas. The farm had nearly two hundred turkeys, geese, ducks and cockerels to be killed, plucked, dressed and delivered to customers in Norchester. With the exception of Eli and Uncle Bart, who were ploughing, and Uncle Jonah, who was attending to the sheep, all the men were engaged on the work. Most of them stood in a row in the barn, plucking feathers from the dead birds. Old Peter, who seemed much more active and lively since he had returned home, was kept busy pushing a wheelbarrow filled with plucked birds across the yard to the big farmhouse kitchen. There Clara's mother and all the other women were dressing the birds and trussing them ready for the oven.

'Talk about a factory!' exclaimed Clara's granny.

Giles was missing. He hated plucking birds and so had persuaded Uncle Jonah to let him help with the sheep. So Clara was left to her own devices. Sometimes she ran across to the barn, where the men, tired of the monotonous work, were pleased to see her and enjoyed teasing her. Her father gave her a sack to collect feathers. She had to gather only the softer, downier feathers in the sack, for they were to be used for filling pillows, cushions, bolsters and feather beds. The stiff quill feathers were collected separately, for making quill pens and spills for cleaning out her grandfather's pipe. When she returned to the kitchen she was sure to find more little jobs waiting for her.

'Lay the table for dinner, Clara.'

'Feed the cats, Clara. I haven't had time to give them their breakfast yet.'

'Clara, go upstairs and fetch your granny's spectacles.'

'More skewers, please, Clara. You'll find them in the woodshed.'

Old Peter fashioned meat skewers out of spindlewood, which he cut from the hedges. He had prepared a good stock of them in readiness for dealing with the Christmas poultry.

On one day, 21 December, when the poultry plucking was nearly at an end, a sack of wheat and a churn of milk were set just inside the kitchen door. It was St Thomas's Day and during the morning people came to the door, 'Thomasing'. On St Thomas's Day, according to custom, poor people could go to their better-off neighbours and ask for food without being accused of begging. Mostly the people who came were women and children. Mrs Emily Franklin, for instance, whose husband had been killed in the wars and who was a very proud lady who would never dream of asking for alms, brought her measure and milk-jug to be filled, just like everyone else. Clara helped her granny dispense the wheat and milk.

Each person had about a gallon of wheat and a pint or so of milk, but the amount varied according to the size of the family. Granny knew them all and so knew how much they needed.

'They're supposed to have enough corn and enough milk to make themselves enough frumenty for Christmas breakfast,' her granny told Clara, 'but they get more than that.'

(Frumenty is a kind of breakfast cereal, popular in the days before breakfast cereals were available in packets.)

A few old men also came Thomasing. To her surprise, one of them was Mr Purdle, the sexton. Clara's granny raised her eyebrows when he arrived, holding out a milk-can and bucket, but she filled them without question.

'He's got a nerve,' said Clara's father, when her granny mentioned it during dinner. 'He didn't offer to pay for the summer keep of his heifer, or the hay he's already bought from me, I suppose?'

'No, he didn't mention anything about that,' said Granny.

Other thoughts were running through Clara's head. When Mr Purdle was going away across the yard something about his movements seemed familiar to her. She thought about it for a time and then, with a start, realized they reminded her of the movements of the man she had seen running away on the night of the turkey raid. And she wondered a lot about Mr Purdle.

On Christmas Eve there were more callers at the farm. They came in several parties, some composed entirely of children but some of grown-ups. After they had sung a carol or two they rapped on the door, calling a message like:

Christmas is coming
The geese are growing fat,
Please to put a penny
In an old man's hat.

The children were given oranges, sweets and cakes, but some of the adults brought a wassail bowl with them. Clara's mother was expecting this and had some mulled punch waiting for them. It was cider to which sugar, raisins, roasted apples, sliced oranges, cinnamon and other spices had been added, and the big preserving pan in which it was brewed was kept simmering over the fire. The wassail bowl was a wooden bowl ('always made of maplewood,' Grand-dad told Clara), about fifteen inches across, with carvings of leaves and berries on the outside. The singers held it out to be filled and then in turn they all drank from it. 'Wassail, wassail,' they cried, which means 'good health'.

Uncle George and Giles had been cutting holly from a bush they had found which was covered with berries, but they were not allowed to bring it indoors till Christmas Eve.

'It would be unlucky,' declared Clara's granny. 'Just as it must be taken out again before Twelfth Night.'

The same applied to mistletoe, a big cluster of which grew on one of the apple-trees in the orchard. Old Peter had fashioned a 'kissing-bush', which is a kind of posy of mistletoe and ivy, for hanging in the hall, but he had to keep it in the woodshed till Christmas Eve.

Christmas came at last. All the turkeys, geese, ducks and cockerels had been delivered to customers in Norchester. Several fat cattle and pigs had been sold in Norchester Market. All the yards and sheds which housed cattle, pigs and laying hens had been littered with fresh straw. Hay, turnips and other rations had been prepared for the animals, so that as little work as possible would have to be done during the Christmas holiday.

'Thank goodness that's finished!' exclaimed Clara's father. 'I'm always glad when we get through Christmas without snow. It makes life so much more difficult when the roads are blocked.'

The weather had, in fact, remained mild, though there had been quite a number of rainy days. On Christmas Eve, however, the storms fled away and left the sky clear of clouds. Mist formed pools in the meadows, and the wet grass was soon sparkling with frost crystals. When Clara looked out of her bedroom window at bedtime after hanging a big pillow-case on the bed-post, she could see the sky studded with stars.

In the morning the pillow-case bulged with something other than feathers. The bulkier part of the contents consisted of apples, oranges, sweets and nuts, among which some unkind person (Clara suspected Giles or Uncle George) had scattered a few holly leaves, to prick her fingers. But there were also quite a number of much better presents. Her granny had given her a fan which she herself had had when she was young—'an heirloom for you to keep' she told Clara later. A golden guinea in a case was a present from her grandfather. Her aunts had bought bracelets, a necklace and brooches. Uncle George's contribution was a fur muff. There was also a piece of cardboard on which were printed the words, 'GO AND LOOK IN THE CUPBOARD BY THE CHIMNEY'. So Clara did and there she found her parents' present, a new red coat with fur collar and cuffs, and a fur-trimmed hood to match. Clara was so overcome with delight she almost cried. She could hardly wait to get dressed and race downstairs to tell everyone about her presents and to thank them all.

During the morning everyone went to church for a Christmas service. Clara wore her new coat and sat between her father and mother in a pew near the front of the church. She hoped that people were admiring her new outfit.

Back at home her father had reserved the heaviest turkey of all for Christmas dinner. It weighed twenty-eight pounds and even then was none too large, for there were fourteen people to be fed. That included old Peter, as well as all the uncles and aunts. Old Peter was living in the cottage where he had always lived, but as he was a widower and had no-one to cook for him he usually came to the farm for at least one meal each day. After the first course, Clara's mother brought in an enormous Christmas pudding, coated with sugar and decorated with a sprig of holly.

'I helped you make that the other day,' Clara whispered to her granny, remembering how almost a month ago she had stirred the pudding mixture in a big basin.

'No you didn't. Not that one. The one you stirred was the one for next Christmas. This one was made more than a year ago. Christmas puddings always taste best if they are kept for a year.'

After brandy had been poured over the pudding and set alight, and the blue flame had gone out, Clara's mother distributed the slices, and everyone started probing their helpings to see what lucky charms had fallen to them. Clara was lucky enough to get a shilling.

'I think your mother knew what she was doing when she gave you that slice,' said her grandfather. Clara thought that was possible, for Giles had a slice with a shilling in it, too. Certainly the other slices were allotted by chance, though, for Clara's granny had the thimble, which signifies that the person receiving it is going to be an old maid.

'And that can't be right,' laughed Granny.

But when Clara's lively and pretty Aunt Miriam, who was married to Uncle Bart, dug the silver image of a baby out of her slice, everybody laughed, and Aunt Miriam blushed and smiled. Clara had been wondering recently about Aunt Miriam, and this seemed to confirm her suspicions.

'Who has the wedding ring?' asked Clara's mother. Everyone laughed again when prim Aunt Martha found it on her plate.

'That's another false prophecy,' whispered Giles to Clara.

Aunt Martha, looking embarrassed, pushed it to the side of her plate.

'It's a good job we don't take such things seriously,' she said.

After the leisurely meal the afternoon was occupied by the domestic and farm chores. While the women were clearing away and washing up the dinner things the men were feeding the farm animals, milking the cows, collecting new-laid eggs from the henhouse and seeing that all the livestock were comfortable for the night. Old Peter brought in more logs for the fire, while Aunt Martha went down to his cottage to make his bed and tidy up. Clara would have liked to go to the village and show her presents to her best friend, Emmie, but her mother said it would be better to leave that till tomorrow, when Emmie and other children would be coming to the farm for a party.

At tea-time a huge candle, two feet high and as thick as a man's wrist, was placed on a decorated bowl in the middle of the table and lit by Clara's father. It was called the Yule Candle, 'Yule' being an old name for Christmas, and it had to burn there without being moved until it had completely melted.

'That won't be till tomorrow,' said her grandfather.

After tea four of the uncles carried in an enormous faggot of wood.

'Here comes the Ashen Faggot!' they cried. 'Make way!'

The faggot was composed of twigs and small branches, mostly of ash wood, because ash wood burns well even when it is still green. It was six or seven feet long, so that it would only just fit on the hearth, and it was bound with withies, which are thin twisted rods of willow.

'Now we'll see who gets married first,' chuckled Grand-dad. 'How many candidates do we have?'

He lined up the unmarried members of the family. They were Uncle Luther, Uncle George, Aunt Martha, Giles and Clara.

'Right, now this withy is Uncle Luther's,' said Grand-dad, pointing it out. 'This one George's, this one Martha's, this one belongs to Giles, and here is Clara's. Now we see in what order they burst.'

Everyone watched with interest as the flames began to creep up through the faggot and the ash wood began to glow. Soon there was a loud crack, as one of the withies snapped and uncurled.

'It's Martha's!' laughed Grand-dad.

'And you had the wedding ring out of the pudding, too,' said Granny.

They all teased poor Aunt Martha who blushed crimson, tossed her head and said it was 'all nonsense'. Then their attention was diverted by another withy bursting, and this time it was Uncle George's. After that, Clara's snapped next, then Giles', and Uncle Luther's last.

'You're evidently doomed to be a bachelor, Luther,' said Aunt Miriam.

'I'm going to be married before you, Giles,' Clara pointed out.

'Who cares?' said Giles.

During the evening they played games—those they played at Hallowe'en and some others as well, including charades. They toasted chestnuts on the hearth and played forfeits, musical chairs, blindman's buff and snapdragon. For snapdragon the lamps were turned low, a screen was placed around the Yule Candle, and brandy was poured into a tray of raisins. The brandy was then set alight, and the players had to snatch as many raisins as they could from the pool of flame. Then Grand-dad told a ghost story, and Uncle Luther gave an exhibition of mind-reading, picking out unerringly any object they had selected while he was out of the room. (This, by the way, is quite an easy trick to play. The one who goes out of the room has a partner who is left inside and knows which object has been chosen. He points to object after object, and the 'wise man' says 'No' until the correct item is reached. What happens is that the two have agreed beforehand that the correct object will be the third one after pointing to, say the table. Simple!) Uncle George was his partner.

'Well, I suppose we'd better take a last look-round,' remarked Clara's father at about nine o'clock. He went out to the back room for his coat and boots and was followed by Uncle Bart and Uncle Luther. Uncle Bart gave his horses an evening meal of hay at this time, while Uncle Luther liked to see that the cows were comfortable.

'We'll have another game of musical chairs,' suggested Clara's mother. 'Or rather, musical cushions. You pass the cushion around while I play the piano.'

They were in the middle of this when Clara's father reappeared.

'You'd better put on your coat and come with me, Clara. I've something to show you.'

Mystified, and helped by her granny, Clara climbed into her outdoor things. Giles decided he was coming too. Clara took her father's hand and the three of them went out into the crisp, cold night.

It was freezing. By the light of the lantern carried by her father Clara could see the frost crystals sparkling on the straw in the yard as they walked over it. The stars above sparkled as though they too were frozen. Clara thought that Aunt Martha would like to get her silver shining like that when she polished it on Thursdays. The stars seemed to be bigger and nearer than they usually were.

Clara's father led them into the big barn. Once inside they made their way along a passage between towering mountains of straw and hay. There was straw underfoot, too, so that their footsteps were muffled. The yellow light of the lantern illuminated the straw walls on either side but could not reach to the roof. Clara knew that up there were great timber beams festooned with cobwebs, but she could not see them. It was as if the stars had been blotted out from the black sky.

Presently they came to a small cavern-like pen with straw on three sides and a rail fence on the fourth.

'The calving pen,' said Clara's father. 'And see what we've got!'

There was Clara's little Jersey cow, Fairy, looking serenely at her through the railings. And, by her side, the loveliest tiny calf!

It was so small that Clara's father could pick it up with one hand, but it was perfect in every way. In the lantern light its creamy-fawn coat shone like gold.

'Oh, the lovely little thing!' breathed Clara.

She climbed through the railings and knelt down to fondle the calf. Fairy, who knew her mistress, looked around approvingly.

'I'll get a bucket of water for the cow,' said her father. 'I expect she's thirsty.'

'What are you going to call the calf?' Giles enquired.

'Oh, I haven't thought of that yet. Let's see, what names are there?'

'Better have something to do with fairies. How about Goblin?'

'No.'

'Brownie?'

'No, I'll tell you what—Pixie!'

The name seemed just right, so Pixie it was.

In another pen across the passage Dandy, the donkey, stood surveying the group. And so, for a minute or two, they all stood, quietly, not speaking, absorbing the scene.

'Well, well, this is a real Christmas scene,' said Clara's father presently. 'The cow, and the ass, and the stable.'

'And a baby in it,' said Clara. 'I wonder whether it was like this, at the first Christmas?'

'It could have been. We'll hope so. It's almost snug enough in here for a real baby.'

'Well, anyhow, this is the best Christmas present I've had,' Clara declared.

11

Welcome to the New Year

The great hall at the farm, which dated from the time when the house had been a medieval manor, was used only on special occasions. At Christmas, however, it was in service for more than a week.

'After getting it all warmed up for Christmas, it would be a pity to let it grow cold again before New Year,' said Clara's mother.

So big logs, some of which needed two men to carry them, were brought in every few hours to replenish the fire on the hearth. Even then it was chilly at the far corners of the room.

This afternoon, the last day of the Old Year, the hall was the scene of great activity. Furniture was moved to allow space for the big oak table, which was wider than an ordinary trestle table and more than twice as long, to occupy the whole of one side of the hall. Along the other side chairs and benches were arranged, and at either end of the table steps were placed.

After the evening meal the guests started to arrive. In addition to the family there were the vicar and his wife, Mr and Mrs Walter Vernditch, Mr and Mrs Harrasmith and their family, Mr and Mrs

Mettish and their family, the Crumps, the Vells, the Offages and old Maria Oxbourne. Even though the hall was large it was quite tightly packed when seats had been found for everyone. There were, in fact, not enough seats for all the children, and Clara, Giles and some of their friends had to sit on the floor.

The band took up their positions at the end of the hall farthest from the furnace-like fire that glowed and flared on the hearth. This was not the full band which played at the May Day Feast, for some of those came from other villages, but there were enough to make plenty of noise. Eli, James and two other men played cornets, Little Tom banged the big drum, old Peter and Joshua Mendip scraped away at their fiddles, and there were also a trombone, a clarionet and Grand-dad with his 'serpent'. When they all played the overture to the performance, after tuning up, the vibrations set the hanging oil-lamps swinging and forced those nearest the music to stick their fingers in their ears.

As the echoes died away Father Christmas entered and climbed the steps to the table-top, which was acting as a stage. He explained that he was quite a newcomer to the proceedings, but the Mummers' Play which they were just about to perform would be exactly as it had been for time out of mind, and would show 'the beloved company' such a fight as they had never seen before. He invited the first champion to enter.

That was St George, who bounded on to the stage, brandishing a huge sword. Shouting loudly, he described what he intended to do to his opponent. He was still boasting when a man with blackened face and a red hat, whom Clara recognized as Saul Offage, the blacksmith's son, jumped up and confronted him.

The two set about each other with their swords and fought a ding-dong battle on the table-top. It was a very realistic fight. The audience cheered, and several times Clara put her hand to her mouth in dismay, because she felt they were going to tumble off the table.

Presently St George dealt the Turkish Knight, as his enemy was called, a tremendous blow which knocked him over. He fell flat on his face and pretended to die. St George began a speech of triumph, but before he had said more than a few words another Turkish

Knight leaped on to the table. A second battle immediately followed, much on the lines of the first. This time, though, it was St George who fell.

As he lay on the stage, presumably dying, Father Christmas rushed in to ask whether there was a doctor present. After he had called twice or three times the oddest figure entered. He wore a shabby frock coat, long trousers which sagged at the knees and were kept up by visible braces, a tall battered top-hat and a red cravat. In one hand he carried a black bag, fastened by a clip, in the other a huge medicine bottle.

'I am Doctor Bendigo,' he announced, 'renowned all over the world from London to Basingstoke. I can cure Hipsy, Pipsy, Palsy, the Plague and the Gout and if you show me a woman seventy years old without a tooth in her gums I can give her a new set as easy as I can heal this knight who lies here bleeding.'

After some more nonsensical boasts he pointed to his medicine bottle which he said contained 'Opliss Popliss drops which would breathe life into the dead.'

More conversation took place, chiefly about how much money he was to be paid. When that was settled the doctor knelt down, seized St George by the nose so that he was forced to open his mouth, and poured the contents of the bottle down his throat. At least, some of the liquid found its way into his mouth, causing him to sit up, spluttering and choking. The rest went over his face, down his neck and over his clothes. It was purple in colour and looked horrible.

'There! That's got him on his feet again,' said the doctor. 'Now, does anybody else need any physic?'

The 'dead' Turkish Knight quickly scrambled to his feet and scurried away. The other had to listen to a speech from St George before he was allowed to go. Father Christmas returned to the stage with a little man in rags and tatters who had ten or twelve rag dolls pinned to his clothes. This, said Father Christmas, was Little Johnny Jack, with his wife and his children on his back. His role was to invite the audience to give generously when the collection box was passed round. He sang a little song in conclusion. It went:

The roads are very dirty, and my shoes are very thin.
I have only a little pocket to put my money in.
Your pocket's full of money, your cellar full of beer.
I wish you a merry Christmas and a Happy New Year.

All the players returned to the stage and sang *Rule Britannia* and *Hearts of Oak*. Then they bowed to the audience, who clapped and stamped their feet, and the play was over.

There was much shuffling and scuffling as everyone prepared to move chairs and prepare for supper, but the vicar stood up and held up his hand for silence. After he had thanked the players he described what the Mumming Play really meant.

It was an allegory, he said. It was a story about a battle between light and darkness. Ever since Midsummer, he reminded them, the days had been getting shorter and shorter, and if the process went on much longer there would soon be no day at all, only one long night. But now, in the middle of winter, the advance of darkness had been halted. From now on the days would grow longer and the sun would return. Our ancestors saw this as a battle between light and darkness. Just as it seemed that darkness had triumphed and St George lay on the point of death, the annual miracle occurred and he was restored to life.

The vicar said a good deal more—indeed, he made quite a sermon of it—but Clara was interested to know the meaning of the play. She saw the point of having it performed on New Year's Eve.

The vicar thanked the players; everyone clapped and cheered again; and then Clara's mother and the other women went to the kitchen to fetch the trays of food that had been prepared. All the actors in the play stayed for the feast, of course. Soon everyone was eating and drinking, and the noise of their chatter was almost as loud as the music of the band. Clara's task was to hand around plates of mince-pies. She had quite a job to prevent Giles and his friends from grabbing the lot.

In the middle of all the conversation and gaiety Clara's father stood up and clapped his hands. People nudged each other and said 'Ssh', and within a minute or so the room was silent.

'As this will be the last time we shall meet this year,' he said with a smile (it was an obvious statement for there were only two or three more hours in the Old Year), 'let me make an announcement of good things to come in the New Year. We are able to look forward to an Easter wedding. Ladies and gentlemen, I have great pleasure in announcing the engagement of my sister-in-law, Martha, to Mr Peter Plackett. I give you the health of the future Mr and Mrs Plackett.'

Everybody seemed absolutely stunned. The announcement had taken them completely by surprise. They didn't know what to say. They all stood up to drink the toast to the health of the couple while Aunt Martha stood by the fire, blushing and playing with her fingers, and old Peter sat on a stool, his eyes fixed on his violin.

Then, one by one, people recovered from their shock and came forward to congratulate the pair.

Clara went to the kitchen to find her granny.

'You didn't tell *me* Aunt Martha was going to marry old Peter,' she said accusingly.

'Nobody knew until a few days ago,' said Granny.

'But they can't get married. They're . . . they're too old!'

Her granny laughed.

'You'd better not let your Aunt Martha hear you say that,' she said. 'She's only just forty.'

'But . . . but old Peter's an old man.'

'Well, to be accurate, he's about sixty-five. I suppose that *is* old to you. It doesn't seem too old to me. Anyway, he's quite active still. He seems to have had a new lease of life since he came home. And older people do get married, you know.'

'I thought if Aunt Martha married anyone it would be Henry Gray.'

'Yes, most of us thought that, too. But when we said so to Martha she was quite indignant. It seems she has no time at all for him.'

'So Aunt Martha will marry old Peter at Easter, and go to live in the little cottage down the road, and old Peter will come to work as usual. There won't be much change, after all, will there?'

'Not much. You'll see almost as much of your Aunt Martha as

before,' her grandmother assured her.

'Shall I have to call old Peter 'Uncle Peter'? That'll sound funny. I think Aunt Martha might have warned us what was going on . . . fancy surprising us like this. When I . . .'

'Ssh,' cautioned her granny, as Aunt Martha came into the kitchen.

'Oh, Aunt Martha,' exclaimed Clara, who could be quick-witted when she tried, 'we were just talking about your wedding at Easter. Can I be a bridesmaid, please?'

'Well, I rather hoped you would,' replied Aunt Martha, with a small smile.

'Oh, good! Thank you!' and she threw her arms around her Aunt Martha and kissed her, something she very seldom did.

For once, Clara was allowed to stay up till the end of the party. She was very tired as midnight approached, but she wanted to see the beginning of the New Year. Just before the grandfather clock struck twelve they all joined hands and sang *Auld Lang Syne*. Then when the chimes died away, they drank a toast to the New Year.

'Outside you go,' Clara heard his father, the blacksmith, whisper to Saul Offage. The tall young man nodded and made his way to the door.

A few minutes later they heard a thunderous knocking at the front door.

'Here he comes. Here comes the first-footer!' somebody called.

Clara's father opened the door, and there stood Saul Offage. In his hands he carried a jar of cider and a log of wood, and under his arm was a loaf of bread. The bread and the cider he gave to Clara's father; the log he carried across the room to the fire on the hearth.

'Here's to the New Year!' people called, and Mrs Harrasmith said,

'Go and make sure the back door's open, to let the Old Year out.'

When she had a chance Clara asked her grandfather, 'What was all that about?'

'Saul was the first-footer,' said Grand-dad. 'He was the first person other than the family to step over the threshold in the New Year.

The first-footer must be tall, dark and handsome. He mustn't be lame, or have a squint or have his eyebrows joined in the middle . . . oh, there are a lot of other things he mustn't be. And he should bring gifts . . . bread, cider and a log for the fire. So he brings good luck for the coming year.'

In bed, just before she went to sleep, Clara thought,

'What an *interesting* year this has been.'

Apart from various adventures she had acquired a new puppy, a lamb which had been exchanged for a lovely little Jersey cow, and now, at Christmas, an adorable calf.

'I wonder what the New Year will be like?' she pondered, sleepily. 'Well, I'm going to have a new uncle—that will be funny—to have old Peter as an uncle—and I'm going to be a bridesmaid, and Aunt

Miriam is going to have a baby, and soon the lambs will be coming again . . .'

Downstairs the back door was flung open, Toby, caught in the act of stealing a turkey's leg, was chased outside with a good scolding and the door slammed again.

But Clara heard nothing. She was fast asleep.